A-LEVEL YEAR 2

STUDENT GUIDE

OCR

Psychology

Component 3: Applied psychology

Issues in mental health
Criminal psychology
Environmental psychology

Molly Marshall

HODDER
EDUCATION
AN HACHETTE UK COMPANY

Hodder Education, an Hachette UK company, Blenheim Court, George Street, Banbury, Oxfordshire OX16 5BH

Orders

Bookpoint Ltd, 130 Park Drive, Milton Park, Abingdon, Oxfordshire OX14 4SB

tel: 01235 827827

fax: 01235 400401

e-mail: education@bookpoint.co.uk

Lines are open 9.00 a.m.–5.00 p.m., Monday to Saturday, with a 24-hour message answering service. You can also order through the Hodder Education website: www.hoddereducation.co.uk

© Molly Marshall 2016

ISBN 978-1-4718-5946-5

First printed 2016

Impression number 5 4 3 2 1

Year 2020 2019 2018 2017 2016

This Guide has been written specifically to support students preparing for the OCR A-level Psychology examinations. The content has been neither approved nor endorsed by OCR and remains the sole responsibility of the author.

Typeset by Integra Software Services Pvt. Ltd., Pondicherry, India

Cover photo: agsandrew/Fotolia

Printed in Italy

Hachette UK's policy is to use papers that are natural, renewable and recyclable products and made from wood grown in sustainable forests. The logging and manufacturing processes are expected to conform to the environmental regulations of the country of origin.

Contents

Content Guidance

Questions & Answers

■ Getting the most from this book

Exam tips

Advice on key points in the text to help you learn and recall content, avoid pitfalls, and polish your exam technique in order to boost your grade.

Knowledge check

Rapid-fire questions throughout the Content Guidance section to check your understanding.

Knowledge check answers

1 Turn to the back of the book for the Knowledge check answers.

Summaries

■ Each core topic is rounded off by a bullet-list summary for quick-check reference of what you need to know.

Exam-style questions

Commentary on the questions

Tips on what you need to do to gain full marks, indicated by the icon ⓔ

Sample student answers

Practise the questions, then look at the student answers that follow.

Commentary on sample student answers

Read the comments (preceded by the icon ⓔ) showing how many marks each answer would be awarded in the exam and exactly where marks are gained or lost.

Section B: options

Option 3: environmental psychology

In Section B every question requires a synoptic response and you must answer all parts of the question.

8 a* Using the research by Black and Black (2007) explain how environmental stressors impact our biological responses. [10 marks]

ⓔ The question injunction is 'explain'. This question assesses AO1 and AO2 skills.

AO1 (5 marks): You must refer to the key study by Black and Black (2007) to access the top band. Knowledge and understanding should be demonstrated through describing the psychological evidence of the key study appropriately and effectively.

AO2 (5 marks): You should apply knowledge and understanding of the Black and Black (2007) study to explain how environmental stressors impact our biological responses. It is important for your answer to make the link between environmental stressors and biological states. An answer that simply describes the study without an explanation will only be awarded marks in the lower bands.

Student A

Research shows that environmental factors may cause stress. One environmental stressor is noise and sudden and unexpected noise produces biological responses of increased blood pressure and increased heart rate. Even when a person is accustomed to an environment in which noise levels are high, physiological changes occur. Black and Black researched the impact of aircraft noise on community health in residential areas near Sydney airport and in a matched control area unaffected by aircraft noise — 750 participants were sent a survey in both the aircraft noise area and in the control area. Also, noise stations were set up outside randomly selected households in the aircraft noise area and in the control area. The survey collected data on health-related quality of life and noise stress and a critical question asked 'Have you ever been told by a doctor that you have high blood pressure?' The research concluded that people who have been chronically exposed to high aircraft noise levels are more likely to report stress and hypertension compared with those not exposed to aircraft noise. This research shows how an environmental stressor, such as aircraft noise, impacts biological responses, and for those who live near an airport, because the noise caused by aircraft will continue, the stress will be long term. Because stress causes raised heart rate and high blood pressure, long-term stress can damage blood vessels which may lead to stroke or heart attacks. Also, the stress hormone, cortisol, can cause damage to health because raised cortisol levels reduce our immune function and also increase the risk of depression and mental illness.

ⓔ 9–10 marks awarded. This is a top-band answer which demonstrates relevant knowledge and understanding. In ■ the student gives an accurate description of noise as an environmental stressor. In ■ the student gives a detailed and accurate

Component 3: Applied psychology 91

■ About this book

This is a guide to OCR A-level Psychology **Component 3: Applied psychology**. It covers the compulsory topic — issues in mental health — and two of the options — criminal psychology and environmental psychology. It is intended as a revision aid rather than as a textbook. Its purpose is to summarise the content, to explain how the content will be assessed, to look at the type of questions you might expect and to consider example answers.

There are two sections:

- **Content Guidance.** This takes you through the material that you need to cover for Component 3: Applied psychology. It outlines the background, key research and application for each topic in issues in mental health, criminal psychology and environmental psychology, as well as providing brief notes on issues and debates in psychology. You need to be familiar with this content as well as with guidance on the different tasks that might be set in the Component 3 examination.
- **Questions & Answers.** This section provides sample questions and answers that are followed by comments and marks. Look at the responses and comments on the responses and try to apply the best techniques to your own answers.

For each of the three major topics the following are provided:

- A synopsis of the topic, background, key research and application relevant to each area. This is not intended as the *only* appropriate content but gives you an idea of what you might include in answer to a question on a particular aspect of the specification.
- Examples of questions in the style of OCR A-level Component 3 exam questions. Each is accompanied by a brief explanation of its requirements as well as the appropriate breakdown of marks between AO1, AO2 and AO3 skills. Synoptic questions are marked with an asterisk (*).
- An example of an A-grade response to each of these questions, showing how the question might be answered by a strong student.
- An example of a C/D-grade response to each of these questions, with comments showing where marks have been gained or lost.

The aim of the guide is to help you to improve your skills in answering the types of question you might encounter in examinations. Author names and publication dates have been given when referring to research studies. The full references for these studies should be available in textbooks should you wish to read about or research the topic further.

Getting started

You will need a file (or folder) and some dividers. There are three major sections (issues in mental health, criminal psychology and environmental psychology) for this component, and within each of these major sections you will need a sub-section for each topic (three in issues in mental health, and six each in criminal psychology and environmental psychology) so you could start by dividing your file into these sections. You should also include a section into which you can put all your assessed work (do not throw it away — keep it and revise from it, rewriting any answers that did not get full marks). You will learn a great deal from this and it would be advisable to keep all this material together.

The specification

Component 3: Applied psychology aims to develop critical thinking and independent learning skills. Each topic contains:

- **background research** — you should be able to explain and exemplify the background and consider relevant issues and debates in relation to the topic
- **key research** — you should be able to describe the key research and appreciate how it relates to the topic
- **application** — you should be able to relate the application of the topic to a novel situation

There are a number of methodological issues and debates that run throughout Component 3 and you must be able to apply these issues and debates across the range of topics, making links between the issues and debates and the content of this component.

You need to learn to:

- describe concepts, theories and studies
- apply methodological issues and debates in psychology
- recognise the contribution the key research has made to the topic
- apply the background, key research and application to novel situations
- consider how different areas of psychology can inform our understanding of applied psychology
- explore social, moral, cultural and spiritual issues where applicable
- recognise how the key research contributes to understanding of individual, social and cultural diversity
- recognise how society makes decisions about scientific issues and how psychology contributes to the success of the economy and society

At A-level, Component 3: Applied psychology is assessed on Paper 3, which is a 2-hour exam, marked out of 105.

On both the AS and the A-level examination paper 10% of the marks available will be for assessment of mathematics skills within the context of psychology. These skills will be at a Level 2 (GCSE level) or higher standard. The specification states that any lower level mathematical skills may still be assessed within examination papers but will not count within the 10% weighting for psychology.

Content Guidance

■ Issues and debates in psychology

Assessment in Component 3 requires you to apply the issues and debates to topics in mental health, criminal psychology and environmental psychology. When answering questions on applied psychology you are expected to illustrate your answers with knowledge and understanding of the methodological issues and debates in psychology. You must understand and be able to apply:

- Nature vs nurture
- Freewill vs determinism
- Reductionism vs holism
- Individual or situational explanations
- The usefulness of research
- Ethical considerations
- Socially sensitive research
- Psychology as a science
- Ethnocentrism
- Validity
- Reliability
- Sampling bias

Issues and debates in psychology: glossary of terms

alpha bias: research tends to emphasise and over-exaggerate differences between cultures (or between genders).

androcentrism: male views and behaviour are viewed as 'the norm' and used to explain both male and female behaviour.

beta bias: research tends to minimise or ignore differences between cultures (and genders).

cultural relativism: the view that beliefs, customs and ethics are relative to the individual within his or her own social context. Cultural relativists believe that all cultures are of equal value.

culture: 'the beliefs, attitudes, social and child-rearing practices etc.' that people of a group share and that distinguishes one group from other groups.

demand characteristics: aspects of the experiment may act as cues to behaviour that cause the participants (and the experimenter) to change the way they behave.

determinism: the assumption that people cannot be held responsible for their actions because their behaviour is determined (caused) by factors outside their control.

ethical guidelines: the British Psychological Society (BPS) has issued a set of ethical guidelines for research involving human participants. These ethical guidelines are designed to protect the wellbeing and dignity of research participants.

ethnocentrism: the effect that your own cultural perspective has on the way you perceive other cultures and people from other cultures.

environmental determinism: the assumption that behaviour is caused by factors outside the individual, e.g. classical conditioning.

external validity: the validity of a study outside the research situation and the extent to which the findings can be generalised (ecological validity).

free will: the assumption that people have the free will to select and decide their own behaviour.

hard (biological) determinism: biological explanations suggest behaviour is caused by genetic factors.

Hawthorne effect: when people are aware that they are being studied, they are likely to try harder on tasks and pay more attention.

holism: the principle that complex phenomena cannot be understood through an analysis of the constituent parts alone, because the behaviour of the 'whole system' cannot be explained in terms of the 'sum' of the behaviour of all of the different parts.

idiographic: comes from the Greek word 'idios' meaning 'own'. Psychologists who take an ideographic approach to psychological investigation want to discover what makes each of us unique.

individualistic/collectivist culture: in individualistic cultures, one's own identity is defined by personal characteristics and achievements, independence and self-identity; in collectivist cultures, identity is defined by collective achievements and interdependence.

internal validity: the extent to which a measurement technique measures what it is supposed to measure, whether the IV really caused the effect on the DV or whether some other factor was responsible.

inter-observer reliability: whether, in an observational study, if several observers are coding behaviour, their codings or ratings agree with each other.

levels of explanation for behaviour: psychologists use four levels of explanation for behaviour — biological processes, basic psychological processes, the attributes of the person enacting the behaviour and sociocultural processes.

nature vs nurture: nature — the extent to which behaviour is the result of genes, biology, hormones, age, gender; nurture — the extent to which behaviour is due to life experiences such as parents or upbringing or culture.

psychic determinism: the type of determinism that suggests all mental processes are determined by the unconscious or pre-existing mental complexes.

reductionism: the principle of breaking behaviour into simple constituents or the use of simple principles, for example explaining complex human behaviour in terms of simplistic single factor causes, such as inherited genes.

reliability: reliability of results means consistency — if something is measured more than once, the same effect should result.

sample bias: participants are drawn from one group, (e.g. students) and then findings are generalised to explain behaviour from different cultures.

soft determinism: the theory that in some situations people do have a choice, but their behaviour is subject to some form of biological or environmental pressure.

socially sensitive research: research into 'sensitive' social issues such as sexuality, child abuse and death, domestic violence, partner abuse and family breakdown. Research is likely to be sensitive if it investigates very personal experiences.

temporal bias: assuming that findings from previous research done many years ago can be applied to explain behaviour today.

validity: the extent to which we can be sure that the research measured the effect of what it 'set out to measure'.

Exam tip

Make your own revision 'dictionary' of key terminology.

▪ Issues in mental health

For each of the three topics you should be able to explain the background and be able to consider relevant issues and debates. You should also be able to describe the key research and appreciate how it relates to the topic area and be able to apply the research to novel situations. Many of the issues and debates can be applied in this topic and you need to be able to answer questions such as 'Discuss the nature/nurture debate in relation to the medical model of mental illness'.

The historical context of mental health

Historical views of mental illness

Mental illness has occurred throughout human history, and its symptoms have always been recognised as unusual or abnormal behaviour. In ancient times, madness was considered a punishment of the gods and in the Middle Ages mental illness was seen as the result of supernatural forces and the blame often fell on witches.

Hysteria and epilepsy were frequently confused with witchcraft or demonic possession. Women were condemned as witches more frequently than men. Women were seen to be more prone to diabolical possession because they were weaker in nature than men and because the uterus was thought to be an unstable organ which could move from one place to another so women, because of their uterus, were innately unstable human beings.

Many cultures have viewed mental illness as a form of religious punishment or demonic possession. Negative attitudes towards mental illness persisted into the eighteenth century, leading to the stigmatisation of mental illness, and often degrading confinement of mentally ill individuals.

Mental health hospitals

In the UK, the institutional care model, in which many patients lived in hospitals and were treated by professional staff, was considered the most effective way to care for the mentally ill. However, mental hospitals were often underfunded and understaffed, and the institutional care system was criticised because of the poor living conditions and human rights violations.

Deinstitutionalisation and outpatient treatment

In the period between the two world wars, talking treatments encouraged outpatient treatment and may have encouraged the idea of shorter stays in hospital. In the 1960s a number of psychiatrists and psychotherapists, known as the anti-psychiatry movement, started to criticise the medical approach to abnormality. Rosenhan was a critic of the medical model and his study 'On being sane in insane places' demonstrates how unreliable psychiatric classification is. By 2000, in place of institutionalised care, community-based mental healthcare was developed to include a range of treatment facilities. While research has reported positive outcomes from community-based mental healthcare programmes, underfunding of community-based mental healthcare has forced the criminal justice system to provide the supervised environment required by a minority of the mentally ill population.

> **Knowledge check 1**
>
> Explain the difference between institutionalised care and community-based mental healthcare.

Defining abnormality

Stratton and Hayes (1993) proposed three ways to define abnormality.

(1) Abnormality as behaviour which deviates from the statistical norm

Some psychologists propose that behaviour is normally distributed. If this is true, then people whose behaviour is very different (more than two standard deviations above or below the mean) can be defined as 'abnormal'. People whose behaviour falls more than three standard deviations above the average will be very rare.

However, the statistical approach accounts for the frequency of behaviour, not its desirability. A very low IQ is, statistically, just as abnormal as a very high IQ, but it is desirable to have a high IQ. Therefore, frequency of behaviour tells us nothing about its desirability. Also, the statistical approach does not allow us to distinguish between rare behaviour that is eccentric (elective), such as keeping snails as pets, and rare behaviour that is psychologically abnormal, such as schizophrenia.

(2) Abnormality as behaviour which deviates from the social norm

Some people behave in socially deviant ways. Because their behaviour does not fit in with social norms or meet social expectations, they are seen as different. For example, a person who scavenges in dustbins and hoards rubbish in their home may be seen as abnormal.

However, this definition could be used to discriminate against people who the majority disapprove of and want to remove from society. Also, whether behaviour is seen as normal depends on its context. Preaching a sermon is seen as normal in a church, but preaching a sermon in a supermarket might be considered abnormal.

(3) Abnormality as failure to function adequately

People who cannot look after themselves, or who are perceived to be irrational or out of control are often viewed as dysfunctional. The problem with this is that it involves others in making value judgements about what it means to function adequately. The individuals themselves may not think they have a problem and their unusual behaviour may be a way of coping with their difficulties in life.

Rosenhan and Seligman (1989) propose seven major features that appear in abnormal behaviour as opposed to normal behaviour. The more of these features that are possessed by an individual, the more likely he or she is to be considered abnormal (dysfunctional):

- **Suffering:** most abnormal individuals (e.g. those suffering with anxiety disorders) report that they are suffering. However, some abnormal individuals, such as those with personality disorders, do not appear to suffer.
- **Maladaptiveness:** maladaptive behaviour prevents an individual from achieving major life goals, from having fulfilling relationships with others or working effectively.
- **Vividness and unconventionality:** vivid and unconventional behaviour is unusual. It is behaviour that differs substantially from the way in which you would expect people to behave in similar situations.
- **Unpredictability and loss of control:** with most people, you can predict what they will do in known situations but dysfunctional behaviour is often highly unpredictable.
- **Irrationality and incomprehensibility:** one of the characteristics of dysfunctional behaviour is that there appears to be no good reason why the person should choose to behave in that way.
- **Observer discomfort:** our social behaviour is governed by a number of unspoken rules about behaviour, such as the way we maintain eye contact or personal space. When others break these rules we experience discomfort.
- **Violation of moral and ideal standards:** when moral standards are violated, this behaviour may be judged to be abnormal or dysfunctional.

One of the problems with using these seven categories is that they rely on subjective opinion and it can be quite difficult to decide which of the features are actually present in a person's behaviour.

Categorising mental disorders

Diagnostic and Statistical Manual (DSM-5), 2013

The DSM-5 contains revised diagnoses and, in some cases, broadened diagnostic definitions while narrowing definitions in other cases. The reliability of categories of disorder was increased by using more precise definitions of each disorder. The DSM is based on a multi-axial system by which an individual is judged on five scales or axes.

Axes of DSM

- Axis 1: clinical disorders
- Axis 2: personality disorders and mental retardation
- Axis 3: general medical conditions
- Axis 4: psychosocial and environmental problems
- Axis 5: global assessment of functioning

Exam tip

In the exam you could be asked to outline one definition of abnormality. Make sure you can do this.

Knowledge check 2

Explain why labelling people as abnormal can be considered as unethical.

Exam tip

Make sure you can list some of the seven features that, according to Rosenhan and Seligman, appear in abnormal behaviour.

Features of DSM

The DSM-5 describes hundreds of mental disorders arranged in various categories. Most of these categories are wide ranging. The disorders are defined by symptoms rather than by features believed to cause each disorder. Each diagnostic category is based on 'typical' sets of symptoms that are believed to be characteristic of that category. Some of these symptoms are essential for a diagnosis to be made, others may occur but are not always present. Some categories are still controversial, such as dissociative identity disorder and dissociative amnesia. Pope et al. (1999) surveyed 301 psychiatrists and found that only about 25% believed that these two categories were supported by strong scientific validity.

Reliability and validity of DSM

A classification system (or diagnosis) cannot be valid if it is not reliable. **Reliability** refers to the extent to which different psychiatrists agree on patients' diagnoses (inter-observer reliability).

Validity refers to the extent to which a classification system measures what it claims to measure. Three kinds of validity are relevant to DSM-5:

- **Aetiological validity:** the extent to which the cause of the disorder is the same for each sufferer.
- **Descriptive validity:** the extent to which individuals diagnosed with the same disorder are similar.
- **Predictive validity:** the extent to which the diagnostic categories predict the course and outcome of treatment.

Exam tip

Prepare to explain why using a diagnostic manual such as the DSM-5 may improve the validity of a diagnosis.

Knowledge check 3

Suggest one way to verify the reliability of a diagnosis of mental illness.

Key research

Rosenhan, D. (1973) 'On being sane in insane places'

Aim: To test the reliability of diagnoses of psychological abnormality. Rosenhan tested this by asking — what if the normal people behaved 'normally' *but* were observed in a psychiatric hospital?

There are three parts to Rosenhan's research.

Part 1 procedure: 8 sane people acted as 'pseudo-patients' (not real). There were 5 men and 3 women of various ages and occupations (graduate student, psychologist, paediatrician, psychiatrist, painter and housewife). Rosenhan was one of the pseudo-patients. No one in the hospitals was informed about the research and the staff and patients in 12 different hospitals in 5 different states across the USA were also 'unaware' participants. The pseudo-patients called the hospitals and asked for an appointment. On arrival they told the admissions officer that they had been hearing voices. When asked what the voices said the pseudo-patients reported that they were often unclear but included the words **'empty', 'hollow',** and **'thud'** (hearing voices is a symptom of schizophrenia). They described the voice as unfamiliar, but the same sex as themselves. They also pretended to be worried about the meaning of life (simulated 'existential crisis'), commenting 'Who am I, what's it all for?' All but one of the pseudo-patients were admitted to hospital and once admitted to the psychiatric ward, they continued to behave as normal. The pseudo-patients took part in ward activities and spent their time **making notes about their experience**. They did not know when they would be discharged and to get out they had to convince the hospital staff that they were sane.

Part 1 results: When they were released it was with the label 'schizophrenia in remission'. This suggests that once schizophrenic, always schizophrenic even if it is 'in remission'. The length of stay ranged from 7 to 52 days (average 19 days). The notes made by nursing staff show that the pseudo-patients were friendly and cooperative, and that they 'exhibited no abnormal indications'. Daily visitors also reported no unusual behaviour, nor did any of the other patients. Some of the patients were keenly aware of the sanity of the pseudo-patients and voiced this loudly: 'You're not crazy. You're a journalist...You're checking up on the hospital.' Normal behaviour was misinterpreted and described by staff as abnormal.

Two examples:
- Writing notes was described as 'The patient engaged in writing behaviour'.
- Arriving early for lunch was described as 'oral acquisitive syndrome'.

This demonstrates how normal behaviour was distorted to fit in with the diagnosis of abnormality.

Part 2: Participants were staff in a hospital who had been informed of the results of the first study. They were told that at some time during the next 3 months, one or more pseudo-patients would attempt to be admitted. Each member of staff was asked to rate all patients for the likelihood that this person was a pseudo-patient on a 10-point scale. During the 3 months 193 patients were judged on the 10-point scale. None of them were actually pseudo-patients but 41 were confidently judged to be pseudo-patients by at least one staff member, 23 were suspected by at least one psychiatrist, and 19 were suspected by a psychiatrist and a staff member.

Part 3: In four of the original hospitals Rosenhan conducted a 'mini-experiment'. The pseudo-patient approached a staff member with a question 'Pardon me, Mr/Mrs/Dr. X, could you tell me when I will be presented at the staff meeting?' or 'When am I likely to be discharged?' As a control, a record was kept of a female approaching staff members on a university campus, and asking them a question. All of the university staff members stopped and answered the question and the respondents maintained eye contact with the questioner. In the case of the pseudo-patients only 4% of the psychiatrists and even fewer nurses stopped and answered the question and most continued without pausing.

Conclusions:
- Doctors were biased and more inclined to call a healthy person sick than a sick person healthy because it is potentially dangerous to release a sick person without treatment (whether they are physically or psychologically ill), so it is better to err on the side of caution. However, this suggests that diagnoses cannot be very reliable.

→

- Diagnostic labels tend to 'stick' even if they are wrong. Once we know someone has been diagnosed with schizophrenia it alters the way we interpret what they do and say.

Rosenhan concluded that: 'It is clear that we are unable to distinguish the sane from the insane in psychiatric hospitals.' In the first study we are unable to detect 'sanity' and in the follow-up study we are unable to detect 'insanity' thus the diagnosis of psychological abnormality appears not to be reliable.

Reference: Rosenhan, D. L. (1973) 'On being sane in insane places', *Science*, Vol. 179 (4070), 250–58

Application

You need to learn the characteristics of three different types of disorder:
- affective
- psychotic
- anxiety

Knowledge check 4

Describe the participants in the first part of the Rosenhan study.

Exam tip

Make sure you can identify one piece of evidence to support Rosenhan's conclusion that psychiatrists cannot reliably tell the difference between people who are sane and those who are insane.

An affective disorder: depression

Clinical depression is a serious condition that affects the lives of millions of people every year. There are two types of depression, unipolar and bipolar, of which unipolar depression is more common.

The characteristics of depression

Depression is a mood or 'affective' disorder in which a negative emotional state colours a person's perceptions, thoughts and behaviour. Clinical depression occurs when depression lasts a long time and affects a person's ability to function normally. Depressive illness is the cause of more than 25% of all deaths by suicide. More women than men are diagnosed with depression (Table 1).

Table 1 Statistics for the rates of depression in the UK, 1993 and 2000

Diagnosis and rate (percentages of population)	Female		Male		All	
	1993	2000	1993	2000	1993	2000
Mixed anxiety and depression	10.1	11.2	5.5	7.2	**7.8**	**9.2**
Depressive episode	2.8	3.0	1.9	2.6	**2.3**	**2.8**

Source: ONS, 2000, *Psychiatric morbidity among adults living in private households in Great Britain*

Symptoms of clinical depression

Diagnosis requires five or more of the following symptoms, including either 1 or 2, for at least 2 weeks:

1 Extreme sadness, tearfulness, depressed mood

2 Loss of interest in, and pleasure in, usual activities and social withdrawal

3 Disturbed sleep, either loss of sleep (insomnia), or more sleep than normal

4 Changed activity level: often agitated, or may be slowed down and lethargic

5   Disturbed appetite and weight change which may be significant gain or loss

6   Loss of energy and tiredness

7   Negative self-concept, including feelings of guilt, low self-esteem and anxiety

8   Difficulty making decisions and diminished concentration span

9   Recurrent thoughts of death or suicide attempts

A psychotic disorder: schizophrenia

Schizophrenia is a misunderstood mental disorder. A person who is diagnosed with schizophrenia does not have a 'split personality'. Schizophrenia is a complex illness affecting a person's thoughts, perceptions, behaviour and ability to communicate. It is a severe and disabling condition.

Characteristics of schizophrenia

The symptoms of schizophrenia are divided into positive and negative symptoms. Positive symptoms are a distortion or excess of normal functions, and negative symptoms are a reduction or loss of normal functions. To be diagnosed with 'schizophrenia' major symptoms need to be persistent, and the diagnosis of schizophrenia requires the duration of two or more of the positive symptoms for at least 1 month.

Positive symptoms

- **Hallucinations:** perceptual disturbances that can be very frightening. A typical symptom is auditory hallucination, such as hearing internal voices. The internal voices may talk about the person, warn them of dangers, or give out orders.
- **Delusions:** disturbances of thought involving false beliefs. There are several types of delusions:
  - **Paranoid delusions:** sufferers may believe that they are being persecuted or conspired against or that people are plotting to kill them.
  - **Delusions of grandeur:** sufferers believe that they are a famous or very important person.
  - **Delusions of control:** sufferers believe that their thoughts are controlled in some way, perhaps that people on television or radio are sending special messages in code.
- **Disordered thinking and speech:** the sufferer may be unable to concentrate or to sort thoughts into logical sequences and communication may be difficult because the sufferer may believe that other people hear his or her thoughts.

Negative symptoms

- **Affective (emotional):** there is a reduction in the range and intensity of emotional expression (flattening of emotion). Also unexpected emotions may be displayed, such as laughing at the 'wrong time'.
- **Poverty of speech:** a reduction in speech fluency and in willingness to talk to others.
- **Reduced motivation:** the sufferer may spend whole days doing nothing, and/or may neglect themselves and appear to lose interest in life.

An anxiety disorder: obsessive compulsive disorder (OCD)

Anxiety disorders occur when anxiety becomes extreme and prevents a person from coping with everyday situations. There are several types of anxiety disorders, including panic disorder, obsessive compulsive disorder (OCD), post-traumatic stress disorder and phobias.

Characteristics of OCD

Obsessive compulsive disorder (OCD) is an anxiety disorder characterised by:

■ recurrent, unwanted thoughts (obsessions)
■ repetitive behaviours (compulsions)

Repetitive behaviours, such as hand washing, counting, or cleaning are to prevent (block out) obsessive thoughts or to make them go away. Performing these behaviour rituals provides temporary relief from anxiety, while not performing these behaviours increases anxiety.

The statistics in Table 2 show that the diagnosis of OCD in the UK has decreased slightly since 1993.

Table 2 Diagnosis of OCD in the UK, 1993 and 2000 (all figures are percentages of the total population aged between 16 and 64)

Diagnosis and rate	Female		Male		All	
	1993	2000	1993	2000	1993	2000
Obsessive compulsive disorder	2.1	1.5	1.2	1.0	1.7	1.2

Source: ONS, 2000, *Psychiatric morbidity among adults living in private households in Great Britain*

The medical model

The medical model explains mental illnesses as caused by biochemistry, genetics and/or brain anatomy. You must be able to describe and discuss the biochemical explanation of mental illness, the genetic explanation of mental illness and brain abnormality as an explanation of mental illness.

Biochemical explanations of mental illness

Neurotransmitters are biochemicals that carry the signals between brain cells. Too much or too little neurotransmitter may result in psychological disorders. For example, too much dopamine is thought to lead to schizophrenia.

Depression: the serotonin hypothesis

Depression is often linked with an imbalance in neurotransmitters. This is supported by the effectiveness of drugs that change levels of neurotransmitters such as serotonin. The World Health Organization (WHO 2001) has concluded that SSRIs are effective as a treatment for severe depression.

Schizophrenia: the dopamine hypothesis

An excess of the neurotransmitter dopamine is thought to be involved because drugs that reduce the levels of dopamine in the brain also tend to reduce the positive symptoms of schizophrenia. Also, drugs like amphetamines that increase levels of dopamine also increase the psychotic symptoms of schizophrenia.

OCD: the serotonin hypothesis

Serotonin is the chemical in the brain that is thought to be involved in regulating everything from anxiety, to memory, to sleep. Medications known as Selective Serotonin Re-uptake Inhibitors (SSRIs) are often used to treat OCD, although it is not fully known why the SSRI medications seem to help some people with OCD.

Genetic explanations of mental illness

Some mental disorders, such as schizophrenia, run in families, suggesting an underlying genetic abnormality.

Schizophrenia

Kety et al. (1994) looked at a sample of adoptees with chronic schizophrenia, and found that the prevalence of the disorder was 10 times higher in the biological relatives of the schizophrenic adoptees than in the biological relatives of the control group.

Gottesman (1991) compiled over 40 studies in order to work out the risks of developing schizophrenia, and found that two classes of relatives have especially high risks of developing schizophrenia — the offspring of two schizophrenic parents and a monozygotic (MZ) co-twin of a schizophrenic.

Gottesman and Shields (1976 and 1982) reviewed the results of twin studies looking for concordance rates for schizophrenia. It was found that in MZ twins there was a concordance rate of 35–58% compared with dizygotic (DZ) twin rates of 9–26%.

Depression

Depression seems to run in families. Close relatives of someone with depression, especially identical twins, have a higher than average risk of developing it themselves.

Harrington et al. (1993) found that a risk factor for depression is having a close relative (parent or sibling) with depression. About 20% of close relatives of people with depression also suffer from depression compared to about 10% of the general population.

McGuffin et al. (1996) studied 177 people with depression and their same sex twins. The concordance rate for depression was 46% in identical (MZ) twins and 20% for non-identical (DZ) twins which suggests that genes are a factor in depression.

Brain abnormality as an explanation of mental illness

Changes in the size and shape of structures in the brain are also thought to contribute to some mental illnesses. Because brain abnormalities have been observed, certain conditions that are considered to be mental illnesses, such as schizophrenia, have been theorised to be neurological diseases. Orlovska (2000) carried out a study based on all Danes born between 1977 and 2000 (1.4 million people) who were followed up to 2010: 113,906 of them had been admitted to hospital with a head injury and 4% of these were subsequently diagnosed with a mental disorder. Also, those with head injuries were:

- 65% more likely to be diagnosed with schizophrenia
- 59% more likely to develop depression
- 28% more likely to be diagnosed with bipolar disorder

Knowledge check 6

Outline a biochemical explanation for any one disorder.

Exam tip

Make sure you can explain what a neurotransmitter 'does'.

Knowledge check 7

Outline evidence suggesting that genetic abnormality causes any one mental disorder.

Exam tip

Make sure you can explain why genes (nature) cannot be said to be the whole explanation for schizophrenia.

Schizophenia: the enlarged ventricles hypothesis

In the normal brain, there is a structural asymmetry between the larger right frontal and temporal lobes. Crow et al. (1993) conducted CT and MRI studies suggesting that left ventricular enlargement means that normal structural asymmetry of the brain is absent in schizophrenic patients.

Evaluation of the medical model

Strengths

- The medical model does not blame people for their abnormal behaviour. It has led to a more humane treatment of the mentally ill.
- The scientific status and association with the medical profession means that this approach enjoys credibility.
- Objective evidence shows that biological causes can be linked to psychological symptoms, e.g. dopamine levels in schizophrenia.

Limitations

- Psychiatrists such as Szasz and Laing object to the medical model. They see the use of labels, such as 'mentally ill', as a way of pathologising people whose behaviour we do not like or cannot explain.
- There may be problems of validity and reliability of the diagnosis because there is frequently a degree of overlap between symptoms of different disorders, meaning the diagnosis may be unreliable.
- The medical model takes a reductionist approach to mental illness. It ignores the cognitive and social factors and the relationship between the mind and body.
- The medical model takes a nature not nurture approach to mental illness, especially if genetic explanations are given suggesting that some people are 'born' to become mentally ill and there is little or nothing they can do about it.

Exam tip

You must able to describe and evaluate the medical model of mental illness.

Key research

Gottesman et al. (2010) 'Disorders in offspring with two psychiatrically ill parents'

Aim: To calculate the risk to offspring of having both parents with a psychiatric disorder. Specifically, to determine the risks in offspring of receiving a diagnosis of schizophrenia, bipolar disorder, unipolar depressive disorder, or any diagnosis from parents who both have received a diagnosis of schizophrenia or bipolar disorder.

Method: The study was a national register-based cohort study in Denmark looking at the risk of schizophrenia or bipolar disorder, calculated as cumulative incidences by age 52 years.

Participants: A population-based cohort of 2.7 million persons born in Denmark, alive in 1968 or born later than 1968, with a register link to their mother and father and aged 10 years or older in 2007.

Results:

■ The risk of schizophrenia in 270 offspring of 196 parent couples who were both admitted to a psychiatric facility with a diagnosis of schizophrenia was 27.3% compared with 7.0%.

■ The risk of bipolar disorder was 24.9% in 146 offspring of 83 parent couples who were ever admitted with bipolar disorder (increasing to 36.0% when unipolar depressive disorder was included) compared with 4.4% with only 1 parent ever admitted and 0.48% with neither parent ever admitted.

■ The risk of schizophrenia and bipolar disorder in offspring of couples with 1 parent with schizophrenia and the other with bipolar disorder were 15.6% and 11.7%, respectively.

■ The maximum risks of any psychiatric disorders in the offspring of parents both with schizophrenia or both with bipolar disorder were 67.5% and 44.2%, respectively.

Conclusions: These patterns suggest genetic explanations for some mental illness and genetic overlap for categories of mental illness.

Reference: Gottesman, I. I., Laursen, T. M., Bertelsen, A. and Mortensen, P. B. (2010) 'Severe mental disorders in offspring with two psychiatrically ill parents', *Archives of General Psychiatry*, 67 (3), 252–57

Knowledge check 8

Does the medical model suggest that nature or nurture is the cause of mental illness?

Application

Treatments based on the medical model assume that mental illness is a symptom of some underlying physical causes. You need to be able to suggest and describe a biological treatment for one specific disorder.

Drug treatments

Drug treatments assume that an imbalance in biochemistry is the cause of the abnormality. Anti-anxiety drugs, such as benzodiazepines, slow the activity of the central nervous system (CNS) reducing serotonin activity and thus anxiety and increasing relaxation. Beta blockers act on the autonomic nervous system (ANS) to reduce activity in the ANS associated with anxiety — these drugs reduce heart rate, blood pressure and levels of cortisol. Anti-psychotic drugs can be used to reduce mental confusion and delusions.

Drug treatment for obsessive compulsive disorder (OCD)

OCD has been linked to low levels of serotonin and/or to increased levels of the neurotransmitter dopamine. **Jenike et al. (1997)** conducted a placebo-controlled trial of fluoxetine (an SSRI drug similar to Prozac) and phenelzine for OCD. In a 10-week placebo-controlled trial 64 patients were randomly assigned to receive placebo, phenelzine or fluoxetine; 54 patients completed the study. There was a significant difference among the three treatments. Fluoxetine-treated patients improved significantly more than those in the placebo or phenelzine group. This suggests that the neurotransmitter serotonin may be involved in the development of OCD.

Drug treatment for depression

Two types of anti-depressant drug are tricyclic drugs and SSRI's (e.g. Prozac). Depression is thought to be the result of having too little of the neurotransmitters serotonin and norepinephrine. Tricyclics work by blocking the mechanism that reabsorbs the neurotransmitters serotonin and norepinephrine, leaving more of these neurotransmitter substances in the synapse. SSRIs work in a similar way, but block the reuptake of the neurotransmitter serotonin. Some side effects of SSRIs may be digestive problems, headaches and insomnia and even suicidal thoughts and aggressiveness.

The World Health Organization (WHO 2001) has concluded that SSRIs are effective as a treatment for severe depression and have fewer unwanted side effects than tricyclic drugs. Fisher and Greenberg (1995) carried out meta-analyses of the use of antidepressants and reported a more than 60% relapse rate among those who responded positively to the drugs and who later ceased to take them, which suggests that the drug was effective. However, Prozac is thought to cause, in some people, an agitated state of mind and an urge to commit murder or suicide.

Evaluation of biological treatment (drugs)

Strengths
- Most drug treatments are effective in relieving symptoms for many people, enabling them to manage day-to-day life.
- Drug treatment only requires that the patient remembers to take the drugs, and does not involve him or her in making much effort or lifestyle changes.
- Drug treatments can be used to relieve symptoms in order to help the patient prepare for another type of therapy, or can be used in a mixture of chemotherapy and other therapy.

Limitations
- Drug treatments do not work for everybody. Individuals can respond differently to the same drug treatments and drug-induced side effects can be problematic.
- Unless there is a clearly understood biological cause for the problem drugs are unlikely to provide a long-term cure. Also, drugs may only provide temporary relief from symptoms, and when the patient stops taking the drugs the symptoms may return.
- Brown (2003) reported that 81% of studies reporting significant findings were published compared with 68% of studies reporting non-significant findings. This bias in publications may lead drug treatments to be perceived as more effective than they really are.

Knowledge check 9

Suggest how a biological treatment can be used to treat one specific disorder.

Exam tip

Make sure you can explain one advantage and one disadvantage of biological treatment for mental illness.

Alternatives to the medical model

In contrast to the medical model, other explanations focus on psychological causes of mental illness. You need to be able to describe and evaluate the **behaviourist explanation** of mental illness, the **cognitive explanation** of mental illness and **one alternative explanation** from the humanistic explanation of mental illness, the psychodynamic explanation of mental illness or the cognitive neuroscience explanation of mental illness.

The behaviourist explanation of mental illness

The behaviourist explanation makes **three assumptions**:

- all behaviour is learned
- what has been learned can be unlearned
- abnormal behaviour is learned in the same way as normal behaviour

This model sees the abnormal behaviour as the problem and not a symptom of an underlying cause.

Behaviourists propose that **classical conditioning** can explain phobias. In classical conditioning, an unconditioned stimulus, such as an unexpected loud noise, triggers a natural reflex (e.g. the startle response and fear). But, if another stimulus (e.g. seeing a spider) occurs at the same time, this may in future elicit the fear response. **Watson and Rayner (1920)** demonstrated how classical conditioning could explain the way in which fear could be learned (the case of Little Albert).

Behaviourists also propose that abnormal behaviour can be learned by the process of **operant conditioning**, in which behaviour is learned through the consequences of our actions. If our actions result in rewarding consequences (positive reinforcement), or in something nasty ceasing (negative reinforcement), we will repeat the behaviour, but we will not repeat behaviour that has bad outcomes. Phobias such as fear of heights can be learned in this way. We become anxious at the thought of boarding a plane, so we decide to go by train and this removes the anxiety (negative reinforcement).

> ## Evaluation of the behaviourist explanation
>
> ### Strengths
> - The approach proposes a simple testable explanation that is supported by experimental evidence.
> - The behaviourist approach is hopeful as it predicts that people can change (relearn) their behaviour.
>
> ### Limitations
> - The approach is criticised as being dehumanising and mechanistic (Heather 1976). People are reduced to programmed stimulus-response units.
> - The approach cannot explain all psychological disorders. Conditioning cannot cure all disorders, e.g. schizophrenia.

Exam tip

Make sure you can explain why the behaviourist approach suggests that nurture, rather than nature, is the cause of mental illness.

Cognitive explanations of mental illness

Cognitive explanations are based on the assumption that people can control how they select, store and think about information. The cognitive approach proposes that dysfunctional behaviour is caused by faulty or irrational thoughts. In the cognitive approach, psychological problems are caused when people make incorrect inferences about themselves or others, and have negative thoughts about themselves and the future.

Beck and Clark (1988) found that irrational beliefs were common in patients suffering anxiety and depression. For example, depressive people often believe that they are unloved, that they are failures as parents, and that nothing good will ever happen in the future. According to Beck (1967) depressed individuals have acquired negative schema during childhood and these negative schema are activated when they encounter any new experience which in turn causes them to 'expect to fail'. Ellis (1975) also proposed that depressed people have persistent self-defeating thoughts that are irrational.

Butler and Beck (2000) reviewed meta-analyses of Beck's cognitive therapy and concluded that 80% of adults benefited and that cognitive therapy was more effective than drug treatment. This supports the cognitive explanation for depression because it shows that if people change the way they think they become less depressed.

Evaluation of cognitive explanations

Strengths
- The approach focuses on how the individual experiences the world and his or her feelings and beliefs rather than relying on interpretations by other people.
- The approach is hopeful as it assumes people have the power to change their behaviour.

Limitations
- The approach may encourage the idea that people are responsible for their own psychological problems, i.e. that they could be 'normal' if they so chose. This could lead to people being blamed for psychological abnormalities.
- The approach is reductionist as it ignores biological causes of psychological abnormality such as genetics or biochemistry.

Knowledge check 10

Outline the difference between the behaviourist and cognitive approach to abnormal behaviour.

Psychodynamic explanations for mental illness

Psychodynamic explanations (Freud) suggest that we experience anxiety when unacceptable wishes originating in the id are only partly repressed and that people with anxiety disorders (e.g. OCD) employ four types of defence mechanisms to reduce their level of anxiety.

- **Isolation:** the patient tries to disown their undesirable wishes.
- **Undoing:** the defence of 'undoing' leads the patient to produce compulsive acts such as hand washing which is symbolic for 'washing away the undesirable impulses'.

- **Reaction formation:** adopting behaviours that are the opposite of the undesirable impulses, such as being obsessively clean and tidy.
- **Regression:** the patient regresses to an earlier stage of development, in which he or she was concerned with controlling bodily functions, to escape their undesirable impulses.

Regression means returning to a stage of childhood in which 'thinking' about a thing may cause it to occur, which may explain why patients with anxiety disorders find their intrusive thoughts so frightening, and why masking these thoughts by compulsive behaviour is so effective in relieving anxiety.

Evaluation of psychodynamic explanations

Strengths
- Apter et al. (1997) assessed adolescent patients, who were suicidal, for ego defence mechanisms and found that the suicidal adolescents scored higher on regression and other ego defences. This suggests that regression may be a factor in psychological abnormality.

Limitations
- If Freud's psychodynamic explanation is correct then psychoanalysis should be an effective treatment, but Salzman (1980) suggested that psychoanalysis may have a negative effect on recovery from OCD because the therapy causes the patient to focus on and to 'think even more' about their intrusive thoughts and obsessions.
- Psychodynamic research usually gathers subjective qualitative self-report data that are difficult to replicate, and may be subject to biased interpretation.
- Evidence for psychodynamic explanations is usually based on case studies and/or analysis of subjective qualitative data which may be biased. Psychodynamic explanations are not scientific.

Key research

Szasz, T. (2011) 'The myth of mental illness: 50 years later'

In this powerful paper, Szasz proposes that people with mental illness should not be seen as victims of biological processes. He argues that psychiatry has become so medicalised and politicised that there is no valid non-medical approach to mental illness, and that the debate about what counts as mental illness has been replaced by political-judicial decrees and economic criteria. In his article, Szasz says that 'the claim that mental illnesses are diagnosable disorders of the brain is not based on scientific research; it is an error, or a deception'. He says that if we accept the scientific definition of illness as the 'structural or functional alteration of cells, tissues and organs' and if all the conditions now called mental illnesses proved to be brain diseases, there

Exam tip

To make sure you understand the key research by Szasz, use your textbook and/or online resources and read his argument in full.

would be no need for the notion of mental illness. In effect, Szasz is saying that if there were biological causes to all 'mental' illness, we would treat these in the same way as any other biologically caused illness. Szasz argues that the term mental illness refers to subjective judgement about the 'bad' behaviour of other people, and that the history of psychiatry is the history of an ever-expanding list of mental disorders.

In his argument, Szasz proposes that, instead of treating people with mental illness with drugs and medical interventions, therapists who respect and understand them can help to reveal the reasons for the abnormal behaviour. He also argues that treatment should only be given to people who ask for help and that 'the public fails to distinguish between counselling voluntary clients and coercing captives of the psychiatric system'. He criticises psychiatry as having become 'a coercive arm of the state' and suggests that modern psychiatric medicine 'threatens to become transformed from personal care into political control'.

Reference: Szasz, T. (2011) 'The myth of mental illness: 50 years later', *Psychiatrist*, 35, 179–82

> **Knowledge check 11**
>
> 'Mental illness can be accurately diagnosed, and successfully treated, in the same way as physical illness.' Outline an argument against this statement.

> **Application**
>
> You need to be able to suggest and describe a non-biological treatment of one specific disorder.

Non-biological treatment of one specific disorder

Treatments based on the behaviourist approach

The treatments proposed by the behaviourist approach are based on the assumption that abnormal behaviour is learned in the same way as normal behaviour and that it can be unlearned. Behaviourists try to identify the reinforcers of abnormal behaviour and change the consequences of behaviour. Behavioural therapies may use:

- Classical conditioning in which an undesirable behaviour can be paired with an unpleasant response (aversion therapy).
- Systematic desensitisation in which phobics can be gradually reintroduced to a feared object or situation.
- Token economies, based on operant conditioning, are often used in schools and hospitals to change the behaviour of delinquents and anorexics.

Treatments based on operant conditioning

Behaviourist therapies based on operant conditioning assume that behaviour that brings about pleasurable consequences is likely to be repeated and such therapies are called behaviour modification. Behaviour modification can involve positive or negative reinforcement. Positive reinforcement means that desired behaviour is rewarded by a pleasant consequence because the use of a reward encourages the likelihood of the behaviour being repeated, for example, if you praise someone for good work you encourage (reinforce) its repetition. Negative reinforcement means that desired behaviour is learned because the consequence of the behaviour is that 'something unpleasant' stops happening (or you escape from an aversive stimulus), thus pleasure is felt.

Systematic desensitisation as a treatment for phobias (anxiety disorder)

Systematic desensitisation is a type of behaviour therapy where the undesired behaviour, for instance a person's phobia, is broken down into the small stimulus-response (S-R) units that comprise it. It involves:

- the construction of a hierarchy of fears
- training in relaxation — the relaxed state is incompatible with anxiety
- graded exposure (in imagination) and relaxation
- homework — practice in real life

For instance, in a phobia of snakes, the least stressful situation might be to look at a picture of a snake and the most stressful might be to have to touch a snake. The therapist works though each S-R unit in the ascending hierarchy, helping the person to replace each dysfunctional response of being afraid, with the response of feeling relaxed. **McGrath et al. (1990)** reported that phobic patients respond to systematic desensitisation and that following systematic desensitisation 70% of patients show improvement in symptoms, but few patients are completely free of anxiety.

Knowledge check 12

Explain the assumption of treatments based on the behaviourist approach.

Evaluation of behaviourist treatments

Strengths
- Behaviourist therapies are effective for treating phobias, obsessive compulsive disorders and eating disorders, and are appropriate for those whose symptoms are behavioural.
- The behaviourist model is hopeful as it predicts that people can change (relearn) their behaviour.

Limitations
- Token economies involving reinforcers that withhold a basic human right, such as food, clothing or privacy, are unethical. These procedures have been ruled illegal in the USA.
- These therapies are only effective for a limited number of disorders — conditioning cannot cure all disorders, e.g. schizophrenia.

Exam tip

You should be able to suggest and explain one limitation of behaviourist treatment for mental disorders.

Summary

You should be able to:
- describe concepts, theories and studies related to:
  - the historical context of mental health
  - the medical model
  - alternatives to the medical model
- apply the methodological issues and debates in psychology to research into mental health
- recognise the contribution of research into mental health issues
- apply the background, research and application to novel situations
- consider how different areas of psychology can inform our understanding of mental health
- explore the social, moral, cultural issues in diagnosing people as mentally ill
- recognise how the research contributes to an understanding of individual diversity
- recognise how research into mental health is useful in society

Criminal psychology

This section looks at how psychology can be applied to topics such as what makes a criminal, how forensic evidence is gathered, how evidence is gathered from witnesses and suspects, the psychology of the courtroom, crime prevention and the effect of imprisonment. For each of these topics you must learn some background theories, key research evidence, and how the topic can be applied to criminal psychology. Many of the issues and debates can be applied in this topic and you also need to be able to answer questions such as 'Assess the methodological issues involved when researching what makes a criminal'.

What makes a criminal? (Biological)

This topic focuses on physiological and non-physiological explanations of criminal behaviour and looks at psychological research into factors and influences that may explain why people turn to crime. At the end of this topic you should be able to:

- describe and evaluate psychological research into the reasons why people turn to crime
- discuss and apply psychological research methods, perspectives and issues to the question of why people turn to crime

Physiological explanations

Are some people 'born to commit crimes', in other words, do people become criminals because of their nature or their nurture? Some research suggests that physiological differences explain why people commit crimes.

Genetic evidence

Brunner (1993): genes and serotonin. The aim of this study was to identify whether there is a link between genetic abnormality and criminal behaviour. It is a case study of 5 males from the same family in the Netherlands. All had committed aggressive violent crimes, including impulsive aggression, arson and rape. All were affected by borderline retardation and demonstrating abnormal and violent behaviour. Urine samples were collected over a 24-hour period and blood samples for DNA analysis. The results found disturbed monoamine metabolism, deficit of MAOA, and mutation on the X chromosome related to excess serotonin. Brunner concluded that mutation in this gene results in monoamine oxidase deficiency (MAOA is sometimes called the 'warrior gene') and that impaired metabolism of serotonin is likely to be involved in mental retardation, which could be linked to aggressive behaviour.

The hormone testosterone

One biological explanation for why people commit crimes is because they are male, because males produce more testosterone which links to behaviour such as aggression, dominance and libido. Statistically, men commit more crimes than women, and most violent offenders are male. **Dabbs (1987)** investigated whether male criminals who had higher levels of testosterone had committed more violent crimes and found that of 11 prison inmates with the highest testosterone levels, 10 had committed violent crimes. Of the 11 inmates with the lowest testosterone levels, 9 had committed non-violent crimes. This suggests that high levels of testosterone may be related to committing violent crimes.

Low levels of physiological arousal

Raine, A. and Lui (1998) suggested that low levels of physiological arousal are a predictor of offending behaviour and carried out a correlational study involving 101 15-year-old boys. They looked for a relationship between a number of physiological measures (e.g. skin conductance, EEG and heart rate) taken at age 15 and the numbers of offences that they had committed by the age of 24 and found a strong correlation between the two measures. Those committing crimes had significantly lower heart rates, reduced skin conductance and more slow wave EEG theta activity than non-criminals.

> **Exam tip**
>
> Make sure you can apply the issue of determinism to the evidence suggesting there is a biological explanation for criminality.

Evaluation of physiological explanations of criminal behaviour

- Physiological explanations are reductionist — they ignore social factors that may influence why people commit crime.
- Physiological explanations are deterministic — they suggest that people cannot use their free will to decide whether to commit a crime, and that if a person is born with a criminal gene or high testosterone levels this will 'cause' them to commit a crime.
- Physiological factors cannot explain all crimes. There are many different types of crime, and while there may be a biological explanation for aggressive and violent crime, there is not likely to be a 'gene' for shoplifting.
- Much of the research into the physiology of crime has methodological flaws or has been carried out on biased samples. Brunner is a case study based on 5 males from one family and this cannot be generalised to explain the behaviour of others. Dabbs' study of testosterone is based on inmates in prison and we do not know whether the levels of testosterone in an all-male prison were the same as when the men committed the crimes. Raine is a correlational study and cause-and-effect conclusions cannot be drawn from correlational analysis.
- Suggesting that crime is caused by nature (not nurture) removes the responsibility for the consequences of crime from the offender, because if people have no free will to choose whether to commit crime they cannot be blamed for doing so.

Non-physiological explanations

Psychologists also investigate non-biological factors that may influence whether a person commits crimes. This section looks at research into the influence of upbringing (social influence) and cognitive factors.

Social factors: upbringing

Some psychological research suggests a nurture approach to why people turn to crime and looks at factors involved in upbringing. Farrington et al. (1996) tested the hypothesis that problem families produce problem children. In a longitudinal study, a group of males was followed from the age of 8 to 32 looking at the association between the convictions of these males to the convictions of their biological parents and siblings. When the participants were age 20, 48% of those with convicted fathers also had convictions compared to 19% of those without convicted fathers, and 54% of those with convicted mothers also had convictions compared to 23% of those with non-convicted mothers. This link remained even when males with both mother and father with convictions were removed from the analysis. These results were confirmed when the participants were aged 40. The results suggest that offending is concentrated in families and tends to be transmitted from one generation to the next.

Social factors: learning from others

Differential association theory states that criminal behaviour is learned during social interaction with others. **Sutherland** proposes that through interaction with others, individuals learn the values, attitudes, techniques, and motives for criminal behaviour. The principles of Sutherland's theory of differential association can be summarised as follows:

- Criminal behaviour is learned.
- Criminal behaviour is learned in interaction with other persons.
- The principal part of learning criminal behaviour occurs within intimate personal groups, e.g. gangs.
- When criminal behaviour is learned, the learning includes techniques for committing the crime as well as the motives, drives and attitudes.
- A person becomes criminal because they adopt the norms and values of the group in preference to the norms and values of non-criminal groups.
- Differential associations may vary in frequency, duration, priority and intensity.
- The process of learning criminal behaviour by association with criminal groups involves all of the mechanisms that are involved in any other learning.

Cognitive factors: rationality

Mandracchia et al. (2007) 'Criminal thinking patterns'

Aim: To identify the defining characteristics of criminal thinking.

Method: Psychometric tests (self-report) and factor analysis.

Participants: Opportunity sample (selected by prison officers) of 435 prisoners in 6 prisons in Texas. Average age 36, age range 18–76. The average sentence was 20 years and the average time served was 5.5 years. The participants were a representative sample of prisoners in Texas state prisons.

Procedures: Participants completed psychometric tests in groups — the test was the Measure of Offender Thinking Styles (MOTS) which measures 77 thinking styles. There are 3 items (questions) per each thinking style, in all 231 questions and the result is analysed by factor analysis.

Findings: Criminal thinking is defined by three thinking styles:

- control: the need for power and control
- cognitive immaturity, e.g. self pity and overgeneralisation
- egocentricity: focusing on self and own needs and wants

Conclusions: Criminals do think differently to non-criminals and the way criminals think can be assessed. Criminal thinking allows self-indulgent and rash behaviour that is contrary to accepted social standards and is irrational, unorganised and subjective and leads to immediate gratification. Criminals can be treated to help them change the way they think and treatment should be offered to first offenders.

Cognitive factors: morality

Are criminals less moral than non-criminals?

Kohlberg developed a developmental theory of moral development based closely on Piaget's stages of cognitive development. Its three levels include pre-conventional, conventional and post-conventional morality. Each level consists of two separate stages.

- **Pre-conventional level:** at stage 1, goodness (or badness) is determined by consequences, so that an act is not bad if one can get away with it. At stage 2, children conform to rules in order to gain rewards, and they will do nice things for other people if they think they will benefit. Stages 1 and 2 compose the lowest level of moral reasoning, in which the focus is on rules and the consequences for breaking them.
- **Conventional (conformity) level:** consists of stages 3 and 4, and corresponds to the age of Piaget's concrete operations. An increased understanding of others' intentions, a decrease in egocentrism, and the desire to win praise from others marks this level. Stage 3 is often called the 'good girl/good boy' stage, when children obey rules to gain praise and focus on the idea that rules should be obeyed because social order and authority are important.
- **Post-conventional (autonomous) level:** the last level of moral reasoning is marked by an internal commitment to an individual's set of values. In stage 5, moral actions are those that express the will of the majority (democracy) but also maximise social welfare. Stage 6 is called universal ethical principles and is marked by a set of self-defined ethical principles that determine right and wrong based on ideas of universal justice and respect for human rights and dignity.

To determine a child's level of morality, Kohlberg paid attention to the reasoning behind the answer rather than the answer itself. For example, having heard the Heinz dilemma, a child might respond that something is wrong because it breaks the law, but it is important to know whether the child thinks laws should be upheld because otherwise one will be punished, or because laws are needed to maintain social order.

In a natural experiment, **Palmer and Hilling (1998)** compared moral reasoning between delinquents and non-delinquents. The sample comprised 126 convicted male and female offenders in a YOI and 22 male and 210 female non-offenders. All were from the Midlands and all were aged 13–22 years old. All participants were given Socio-Moral Reflection Measure-Short Form (SRM-SF), which contains 11 moral dilemma-related questions (e.g. not taking things that belong to others and keeping a promise to a friend). The delinquent group showed less mature moral reasoning. In the male groups there was a difference on 10 out of 11 questions and in the female group it was 7 out of 11.

Evaluation of non-physiological explanations of criminal behaviour

- Some social explanations of crime are deterministic — they suggest that people cannot use their free will to decide whether to commit a crime, and that if a person is born into a certain type of family they will become a criminal.
- Cognitive factors such as morality cannot explain all crimes, there are many different types of crime, and while most murders are seen as 'immoral' some would argue that 'assisting suicide' is a moral decision.
- It is hard to gain a valid measure of 'thought patterns' and we can never be sure that measures of thinking styles in prisoners reflect the way the offenders were thinking when they committed the crime.
- Much of the research into causes of crime is longitudinal, and the longer a study continues, the less certain it is that the variable of interest 'caused' the criminal behaviour.
- Suggesting that crime is not caused by nurture (upbringing) removes the responsibility for the consequences of crime from the offender, because even if one's parent is a criminal, offspring have the free will to choose whether to commit crime.

Exam tip

Individual or situational explanation for criminality? Make sure you can explain how social and cognitive explanations differ.

Knowledge check 13

List two social factors and two cognitive factors thought to explain criminality.

Key research

Raine et al. (1997) 'Brain abnormalities in murderers indicated by positron emission tomography'

Research suggests that brain dysfunction may predispose a person to being violent. The pre-frontal area of the brain has been associated with impulsivity. Damage to the hippocampus and amygdala have been associated with aggressive behaviour, and damage to the corpus callosum has been associated with a predisposition to violence. Some violent offenders plead not guilty by reason of insanity (NGBI) to murder charges.

Hypothesis: That the seriously violent individuals have localised brain damage in the prefrontal cortex, the amygdala, the thalamus or the hippocampus.

Participants: 41 murderers (39 males 2 females) all charged with murder/manslaughter in California/USA. All pleaded NGBI and were referred for physiological examination.

- **'Histories':** 23 head injury/brain damage, 3 drug abuse, 2 affective disorder, 2 epilepsy, 3 hyperactivity and learning impairment, 2 personality disorder.

- **Control group:** 41 normal individuals (non-murderers) matched for sex and age including 6 schizophrenics who were matched with 6 'murderer' schizophrenics.
- **Not controlled:** 6 murderers were left handed, 14 murderers were non-white, 23 murderers had a history of head injury.

Research method: A quasi experiment.

Procedure: PET scans to examine the brain (PET stands for positron emission tomography and this method measures the amount of metabolic activity in various parts of the brain). During the PET scan the participants engaged in a 'continuous activity' designed to activate the frontal lobes, right temporal and parietal lobes.

Results: There were differences in the brains of the murderers:

- lower activity in the cortical regions and subcortical regions
- reduced activity in the prefrontal cortex and parietal region
- reduced activity in the corpus callosum
- left hemisphere less activity than right
- abnormal asymmetries in amygdala and thalamus
- both groups performed similarly on performance task

Conclusion: It is unlikely that violence is due to a single brain mechanism but there is some evidence that murderers pleading NGRI may have different brain functions from 'normal' people. These findings do not demonstrate that violent behaviour is 'caused' by biology or that murderers are not responsible for their actions, but they do suggest there may be a link between brain activity and a predisposition towards violence which should be investigated further.

Reference: Raine, A., Buchsbaum, M., and LaCasse, L. (1997) 'Brain abnormalities in murderers indicated by positron emission tomography', *Biological Psychiatry*, 42 (6), 495–508

> **Knowledge check 14**
>
> Outline how the findings of the Raine et al. (1997) research suggest a biological explanation for violent crime.

> **Exam tip**
>
> You could be asked to discuss whether crime is caused by nature or nurture. Make sure you can identify and explain the evidence of physiological and non-physiological causes of criminal behaviour.

Biological strategies for preventing criminal behaviour

> **Application**
>
> You need to be able to describe and evaluate at least one biological strategy for preventing criminal behaviour. Since gene therapy is not yet possible drug therapy seems to be the most useful biological strategy. Two examples of possible drug treatments are given below.

Drug treatment for criminality associated with ADHD

Lichtenstein et al. (2012)

Introduction: Medication treatment for ADHD has been shown to reduce criminality in adults with ADHD.

Method: Information was collected on 25,656 patients with a diagnosis of ADHD, their pharmacologic treatment, and subsequent criminal convictions in Sweden from 2006 through to 2009. A comparison was made of the rate of criminality while the patients were receiving ADHD medication, as compared with the rate for the same patients while not receiving medication.

Results: As compared with non-medication periods, among patients receiving ADHD medication, there was a significant reduction of 32% in the criminality rate for men and 41% for women. During treatment periods the likelihood of being convicted of a crime was approximately 30% lower for men and 22% lower for women.

Conclusion: These findings suggest that the use of medication reduces the risk of criminality among patients with ADHD.

Drug treatment for criminality associated with high levels of testosterone

P. T. Loosen et al. (1994)

Attempts to reduce aggression and sexual predation in male sex offenders have included surgical castration and chemical castration (the use of female hormones to suppress testosterone levels). Research shows that mild reductions in testosterone levels can significantly reduce male aggression. Loosen et al. (1994) suppressed the testosterone levels in eight normal men and found that they all showed marked reductions in outward-directed anger during the experiment, while half exhibited reductions in anxiety and sexual desire.

> **Exam tip**
>
> You could be asked to discuss the ethical issues involved in biological treatments for criminal behaviour.

Collection and processing of forensic evidence (Biological)

You need to know about motivating factors and bias in the collection and processing of forensic evidence, be able to describe key research into whether emotional context affects fingerprint analysis, and to apply this knowledge, and suggest at least one strategy for reducing bias in the collection and processing of forensic evidence.

Motivating factors and bias in the collection and processing of forensic evidence

Cognitive bias occurs when inferences about other people and situations are made in an illogical fashion. In forensic science the consequences of cognitive bias may influence whether or not to prosecute a person. Some of the cognitive biases that may affect the collection and processing of forensic evidence are:

- **Expectation bias:** occurs when investigators disbelieve or downgrade the significance of findings that conflict with their original expectations, while certifying material that supports pre-existing expectations.
- **Confirmation bias:** in the evaluation of DNA mixtures, if the reference sample is compared before the crime profile has been interpreted, confirmation bias would result if the analyst looked only for features supporting the inclusion of the reference profile within the mixture.
- **Anchoring effects:** investigators may fix too readily on a specific subject early on in an investigation and look to explain the circumstances around that person, while ignoring alternative explanations.

- **Contextual bias:** a scientist working within a police laboratory could be influenced by knowing that detectives believe they have a strong suspect, or that the suspect has already confessed to having committed the crime.
- **Role effects:** happen when scientists identify themselves within adversarial judicial systems as part of either the prosecution or defence teams. This may introduce subconscious bias which can influence decisions especially where some ambiguity exists.
- **Motivational bias:** may happen in serious crimes when the scientist wants the police to 'win' and when in doubt will always make a decision in one direction.

Read more on 'Forensic Science Regulator: Overseeing Quality' at www.tinyurl.com/hraywuw.

Research evidence

Example of where cognitive bias became an issue: the Brandon Mayfield case 2006

Brandon Mayfield, an Oregon attorney, was arrested by the FBI as a material witness in an investigation of terrorist attacks on commuter trains in Madrid because the FBI fingerprint department had conducted a database search of a fingerprint found on a bag of detonators and identified it as belonging to Brandon Mayfield. Two weeks after Mayfield's arrest, the Spanish National Police informed the FBI that they had identified the print to an Algerian national called Daoud. The FBI compared Daoud's prints with the impression on the bag of detonators, agreed the findings and withdrew their previous identification of Mayfield. The US Department of Justice reviewed the case and suggested that the examiners applied a lower level of scrutiny to the information which supported their 'favoured hypothesis of identification' and that the examiners seemed to be 'unconsciously seeking out information to confirm their favoured hypothesis' of identification.

Motivating factors in the processing of fingerprint evidence

Within fingerprint bureaus, the majority of examination requests are received from police officers or prosecution services, with both hoping that the examination outcomes will help solve the case or secure a conviction. Contributing to the detection of crime is considered a fundamental aspect of fingerprint bureau service delivery. Also, personal identification or 'hit rates' are used as key performance indicators at both organisational and individual level. The desire to increase their 'hit rate' may motivate investigators (and may cause bias) to identify fingerprints.

Charlton et al. (2010)

The aim of the research was to investigate the factors that relate to the latent fingerprint examiner's experience. The study investigated the **emotional and motivational factors** involved in fingerprint analysis in day-to-day routine case work and harrowing criminal investigations. Thematic analysis was performed on interviews with 13 experienced fingerprint examiners from a variety of law enforcement agencies.

The participants included those involved in the investigation of daily volume crime such as burglary and vehicle theft, and others who dealt with the more rare investigations of rape, murder or armed robbery. The broad range of the participant's

Exam tip

Prepare to suggest how cognitive bias can influence the processing of forensic evidence.

experiences decreased the chance of deriving participant or role specific themes. All participants were fully trained and performed fingerprint comparison analysis daily. Each interview lasted approximately 30 minutes. The findings revealed the following motivational factors:

- job satisfaction
- the use of skill
- satisfaction related to catching criminals
- solving high-profile, serious, or long-running cases.

There were positive emotional effects associated with matching fingerprints and apparent fear of making errors. Also, there was evidence for a need of closure in fingerprint examiner decision making.

The researchers concluded that fingerprint examiners are emotionally driven and motivated to achieve results for themselves, their employees, the police and society. There are subtle psychological factors such as need for closure that influence the decision-making thresholds of examiners that may, in the right circumstances, lead to erroneous conclusions should the context and the motivation be strong enough.

> **Exam tip**
>
> Make sure you can suggest how emotional motivation bias may influence fingerprint analysis.

Key research

Hall, L. J. and Player, E. (2008) 'Will the introduction of an emotional context affect fingerprint analysis and decision making?'

Fingerprint identification relies on an expert's ability to recognise differences and similarities in friction ridge detail accurately, but it has been suggested that the interpretation and analysis of fingerprints becomes more subjective as clarity decreases and as a consequence the expert is more vulnerable to external stimuli. Research involving 70 fingerprint experts was conducted to establish whether the introduction of an emotional context (e.g. murder or robbery) would alter the experts' judgement of an ambiguous or poor quality mark. The emotional context did have a perceived effect on the experts' analysis, as more stated they were affected by the information they were given. However, it did not have any actual effect on their final opinions as no difference was observed between the high and low emotional contexts.

Reference: Hall, L. J. and Player, E. (2008) 'Will the introduction of an emotional context affect fingerprint analysis and decision making?', *Forensic Science International*, 181 (1), 36–39

> **Knowledge check 15**
>
> Suggest how motivation bias could influence fingerprint analysis.

> **Exam tip**
>
> This is a key study. You must be able to outline the study and explain how it can be applied. Use your textbook or online resources to search for and read the research in more depth.

Strategies for reducing bias in the collection and processing of forensic evidence

> **Application**
>
> You need to be able to describe and evaluate at least one strategy for reducing bias in the collection and processing of forensic evidence.

Bias countermeasures (also known as 'debiasing techniques')

Blinding precautions: providing the forensic examiner only with information about the case that is required in order to conduct an effective examination is the most powerful means of safeguarding against the introduction of contextual bias. The FBI has defined blind verification as the independent application of analysis, comparison and evaluation (ACE) to a fingerprint by another examiner who does not know the conclusions of the primary examiner. Blind verifications cannot be performed by any examiner who has knowledge of the previous examiner's conclusions, or specific case details.

Independent checking: good practice in forensic science requires that independent checking of critical findings is undertaken. Independent checking that minimises the risk of cognitive bias entails assessment without knowing the outcome of the initial analysis, or, to avoid confirmation bias, the identity of the original examiner.

Structured approach to the analysis of forensic evidence

The application of a structured approach to performing a comparison and arriving at a decision using a step-by-step linear process can effectively reduce or eliminate the influence of the target (i.e. information pertaining to suspect) from the conclusions drawn. A good example of a general methodology for undertaking comparisons is **analysis, comparison, evaluation and verification (ACE-V)**.

It is the most commonly accepted approach to fingerprint comparison in the UK and USA. The sequence of working is:

- analysis — an examiner analyses a mark
- comparison — the examiner then compares the mark to a known print
- evaluation — having compared the images, the examiner evaluates what they have seen and reaches a decision
- verification — the results are then subject to verification by one additional examiner or more

The ACE-V process is in fact not linear in application to fingerprint comparisons because the analysis phase can be revisited in a well-structured way during the comparison phase. However, the evaluation is a separate stage as described.

Collection of evidence (Cognitive)

For this topic you need to understand how information is collected from witnesses and suspects (Table 3), be able to describe how the cognitive interview is used, as well as being able to evaluate the review of the cognitive interview. In the applied section you need to be able to suggest at least one strategy for improving police interviews.

Table 3 Differences between interviewing a witness and interrogating a suspect

Interview	Interrogation
Purpose is to gather information	Purpose is to get a confession
Non-accusatory	Accusatory
Free flowing	Structured
Suspect speaks most of the time	Suspect speaks for little of the time
Varied locations	Interrogator has 'home field' advantage

> **Knowledge check 16**
>
> List three ways to reduce the influence of motivational bias in fingerprint analysis.

> **Exam tip**
>
> You could be asked to suggest how to reduce bias in the collection of forensic evidence, so you should practise writing an answer on this.

Collection of evidence from witnesses

There are various ways to interview a witness, and psychologists have researched which interview type is most effective:

■ Standard interview — although it could be argued that the standard interview is not standardised.

■ Guided memory interview — the witness is guided step-by-step through the incident and asked to describe the incident, the environment and their emotional reactions.

■ Structured interview — the interviewer tries to build rapport with the interviewee and allows time for the narrative to develop, interrupting as little as possible.

■ The cognitive interview — the interviewer aims to use a variety of techniques to stimulate detailed recall of the event.

The cognitive interview

The cognitive interview is a method of eliciting evidence from witnesses using methods based in cognitive psychology. Working on the basis that memory is associative and that retrieval of an event is more effective if situated within the context of its occurrence, the cognitive interview aims to use a variety of techniques to stimulate detailed recall of the event. **Fisher et al. (1989)** suggested that using the cognitive interview results in a 30% improvement in recall, with no increase in the number of incorrect responses.

The cognitive interview technique involves:

■ mentally reinstating the context of the event, i.e. the sounds, smells, feelings experienced during the event

■ asking witnesses to recall the event in various orders or in reverse order

■ asking witnesses to report absolutely everything, regardless of the perceived importance of the information

■ recalling the event from a variety of perspectives, e.g. imagining what the scene must have looked like from the point of view of several characters there at the time

Each of these retrieval techniques allows the witness to review the event without the interference of leading questions but forces them to scrutinise their memory record. The technique aims to maximise the number of potential retrieval routes and to benefit from overlaps, hopefully triggering otherwise forgotten details of the event.

Collection of evidence from suspects

Recognising deception

When police are interviewing a suspect what they really want is a confession so it is useful if they can tell whether the suspect is telling the truth or not. However, research by Vrij et al. suggests that the police are not much better than the rest of us at recognising deception.

Vrij, A. and Mann, S. (2001)

Aim: To examine the ability of police officers to detect deception.

Sample: 52 uniformed police officers from the Netherlands.

Knowledge check 17

Outline two reasons why a cognitive interview may be more effective than a standard interview.

Exam tip

To help you prepare for a question on the cognitive interview look up and read more about the research by Fisher et al. (1989).

Method: 8 short clips from videotaped press conferences where people were asking the general public for help in finding their relatives or the murderers of their relatives — 5 of the clips were of people who had later been convicted of the crime and 3 clips were assumed to contain no deception. The officers had to watch each clip and then indicate:

- whether they thought the person was lying YES/NO
- how confident they were with their decision (1–7 scale)
- whether they could understand what the person was saying (clips were in English) YES/NO
- any behavioural cues that prompted their decisions

Findings: 49 of the 52 officers did no better than would have been expected by simply guessing. Age, length of service, level of experience in interviewing suspects and confidence had no effect on the accuracy scores.

Conclusion: That detecting deception is a difficult task at which even police officers are not very good.

Interrogation techniques

The purpose of an interrogation is to extract a confession from a suspect. Many forces use interrogation manuals written by experienced interrogators. Interrogation methods involve deception, manipulation, pressure and persuasion.

Pearce and Gudjonsson (1999) analysed recordings from 18 serious crimes and found that the police tend to use six tactics in interrogations:

- intimidation, e.g. emphasise the experience of the police officer
- robust challenge, e.g. accuse suspect of lying
- manipulation, e.g. minimise seriousness of offence
- leading questions
- reassurance, e.g. appeal to the suspect's good character
- soft challenge, e.g. allow suspect's version of events and speak quietly

Intimidation and robust challenge were the most frequently used tactics.

> **Knowledge check 18**
>
> List three techniques used during interrogation.

Key research

Memon, A. and Higham, P. A. (1999) 'A review of the cognitive interview'

The research is an analysis of laboratory studies of the cognitive interview (CI) together with an empirical meta-analysis summarising 25 years of research. The study space comprised 57 published articles (65 experiments) on the cognitive interview, providing an assessment of the boundary conditions underlying the analysis and application of this interview protocol.

Studies: The studies that were considered for inclusion in the study were primarily obtained via searches of online databases. A total of 57 published articles (65 experiments) that empirically assessed the effectiveness of the CI were located.

→

Inclusion/exclusion criteria: To be included in the study, studies must have conducted an experimental analysis of the cognitive interview in comparison to a control or other interview protocol. In addition, the research had to be published in a peer-reviewed journal.

Coding of studies: For each study, the independent and dependent variables were identified and listed in an individual matrix. For example, the independent variables included type of interview (enhanced cognitive interview vs structured interview), retention interval (4 hours vs 6 weeks) and age of witness (8–9 vs 11–12 year olds). The dependent variables included total correct recall, total incorrect recall and total confabulations, and each of these were split into type of detail (i.e., action, person and object details).

Control or comparison group: Whereas early studies of the CI tended to use a standard interview as a comparison (21%), more recent studies (69%) refer to a structured interview control.

Findings: The findings of the original meta-analysis were replicated with a large and significant increase in correct details and a small increase in errors. In addition, the research found that there were no differences in the rate at which details are confabulated. Importantly, the effect sizes were unaffected by the inclusion of recent studies using modified versions of the cognitive interview. The cognitive interview appeared to benefit older adult witnesses even more than younger adults.

Conclusion and application: Training in the use of the cognitive interview is important because training can improve the confidence and ability of a police officer when it comes to using the cognitive interview. The cognitive interview takes longer to administer, and involves instructing witnesses in the use of techniques such as context reinstatement. Interviewers need the social skills to communicate effectively with witnesses and need to develop rapport with witnesses before the interview starts.

Reference: Memon, A. and Higham, P. A. (1999) 'A review of the cognitive interview', *Psychology, Crime and Law*, 5 (1–2), 177–96

> **Exam tip**
>
> In an exam you could be asked to discuss the Memon and Higham (2008) review of the cognitive interview, so make sure you are able to explain one strength and one weakness of it.

Application

You should be able to suggest and describe at least one strategy for the police to use when interviewing witnesses and be able to explain why this strategy may be effective.

> **Knowledge check 19**
>
> Outline the conclusions of the Memon and Higham review of the cognitive interview.

Psychology and the courtroom (Cognitive)

You need to be able to describe research into how juries can be persuaded by the characteristics of witnesses and defendants, describe the key research by Dixon et al. (2002) 'The role of accent and context in perceptions of guilt', and suggest and explain at least one strategy to influence jury decision making.

The persuasive characteristics of witnesses

Stewart, J. E. (1985)

This research looked into a correlation between the attractiveness of a defendant and the severity of the punishment awarded.

Participants: 60 criminal trials were observed in Pennsylvania, USA. Eight observers were used (all white) and each was given a standard rating form. Each trial was observed by at least two observers.

Method: Observers rated the defendants on a range of scales. These included physical attractiveness, neatness, cleanliness and quality of dress. These four items were combined to produce an attractiveness index. Several other ratings were also done — the most important of these was posture.

Findings: No significant correlation was found between race and attractiveness index and the inter-rater reliability for observer ratings was high (.78). However, the less attractive the defendants were judged to be the more severe their punishment was. The fifth item, posture, also showed this negative correlation.

Knowledge check 20

Does the term 'the persuasive characteristics of witnesses' refer to situational or dispositional characteristics?

Key research

Dixon et al. (2002) 'The role of accent and context in perceptions of guilt'

Does it matter if witnesses or suspects speak with a regional accent? Speaking immediately reveals something about social and cultural identity and research shows that attitudes and stereotypes are transmitted by skin colour, names or physical attractiveness, and by accent perception.

This independent group design study by Dixon et al. examined the effect of regional accent on the attribution of guilt. The regional accent investigated was 'Brummie' (Birmingham) which is generally perceived as low status.

One hundred and nineteen participants listened to a 2 minute recorded exchange between a British male criminal suspect and a male policeman. Employing the 'matched-guise' technique, this exchange was varied to produce
- two accent types: Birmingham/standard
- two races of suspect: black/white
- two crime types: blue collar/white collar

In each condition the listener was asked to judge whether the speaker was guilty of the crime.

The results suggested that the suspect was rated as significantly more guilty when he employed a Birmingham rather than a standard accent. The condition in which the male suspect was a black Brummie was judged to be guilty more than the 'non-Brummie' condition. Also, attributions of guilt were significantly associated with the suspect's perceived superiority and social attractiveness.

Reference: Dixon, J.A., Mahoney, B., Cocks, R. (2002) 'Accents of guilt effects of regional accent, race, and crime type on attributions of guilt', *Journal of Language and Social Psychology*, 21 (2), 162–68

Exam tip

In the exam you may be asked to discuss methodological issues, so make sure you can explain whether the research by Dixon et al. (2002) has high or low external validity.

> **Application**
>
> You need to be able to suggest and explain at least one strategy to influence jury decision making. For example, you can see from the Loftus research, that if the prosecution has an eyewitness, even a weak eyewitness, presenting their evidence may influence the jury.

Loftus (1974) 'How important is eyewitness evidence in the minds of jurors?'

Loftus presented 150 mock jurors with a scenario about a robbery and murder in a local store. There were three experimental conditions:

- Condition 1: an eyewitness said he saw a man leaving the store: In this condition 72% of mock jurors found the defendant guilty.
- Condition 2: there was no eyewitness evidence and only 18% of mock jurors found the defendant guilty.
- Condition 3: there was an eyewitness but his evidence was discredited because it was established that he was short-sighted, and not wearing his spectacles at the time of the offence, and so could not have seen the robber's face from where he was standing. In this condition 68% of mock jurors found the defendant guilty.

From this we can conclude that producing an eyewitness has a powerful influence on jury decision making.

> **Exam tip**
>
> Make sure you can explain the methodological issues that arise when investigating jury persuasion.

Crime prevention (Social)

For crime prevention you need to be able to describe research into how the features of neighbourhoods and a zero tolerance policy can influence crime and describe the 'broken windows' research by Wilson and Kelling (1982). You must also be able to suggest and explain at least one strategy for crime prevention.

How the features of neighbourhoods and a zero tolerance policy can influence crime

Crime prevention and defensible space

Newman (1972) suggests that crime and delinquency can be controlled and mitigated through environmental design. The defensible space theory proposes that people in a community help with crime prevention because they protect spaces they feel they have invested in — an area is safer if the people who live in it feel a sense of ownership and responsibility towards the area. Broken windows and vandalism occur because communities do not care about the damage. According to Newman, defensible space is 'a residential environment whose physical characteristics, building layout and site plan, function to allow inhabitants themselves to become key agents in ensuring their security'. Newman asserts that when each space in an area is owned and cared for by a responsible party criminality is reduced because if an intruder senses a watchful community, he feels less secure committing his crime. There are five factors that make a defensible space:

- territoriality — the idea that one's home is sacred
- natural surveillance — the link between an area's physical characteristics and the residents' ability to see what is happening
- image — the capacity of the physical design to impart a sense of security
- milieu — other features that may affect security, such as proximity to a police substation or busy commercial area
- safe adjoining areas — for better security, residents obtain a higher ability of surveillance through designing the adjoining area

Zero tolerance policing

Zero tolerance is a policing strategy that involves relentless order maintenance and aggressive law enforcement against even minor crimes and incivilities. The strategy is based on the 'broken windows' theory, according to which there is a link between disorder and crime because visible signs of decay like broken windows, graffiti and abandoned housing signals public disinterest. Fear of crime is greatest in these neighbourhoods, which prompts 'respectable' community members to leave so decline follows. The zero tolerance theory demands that even minor misdemeanours must be pursued with the same vigour as serious crimes because it is easier to prevent a neighbourhood's slide into crime than to rescue it.

Example of zero tolerance policing in New York

New York City police commissioner William Bratton was convinced that the aggressive order-maintenance practices of the New York City police department were responsible for the dramatic decrease in crime rates within the city during the 1990s. Bratton translated the theory into practice as the chief of New York City's transit police from 1990 to 1992. Squads of plainclothes officers were assigned to catch turnstile jumpers, and, as arrests for misdemeanours increased, subway crimes of all kinds decreased dramatically. In 1994, when he became New York City police commissioner, Bratton introduced his broken windows-based 'quality of life initiative'. This initiative cracked down on disorderly behaviour, public drinking, street prostitution and unsolicited windshield washing or other such attempts to obtain cash from drivers stopped in traffic. When Bratton resigned in 1996, felonies were down almost 40% in New York, and the homicide rate had been halved.

Key research

Wilson, J. Q. and Kelling, G. L. (1982) 'The police and neighbourhood safety: broken windows'

If a building has broken windows that are not repaired the tendency is for vandals to break a few more and eventually they may even break into the building, and perhaps become squatters or light fires inside. Wilson and Kelling suggest that to reduce crime, problems must be fixed when they are small, because if broken windows are repaired quickly vandals are much less likely to break more windows or do further damage and because problems do not escalate respectable residents do not leave a neighbourhood. →

Knowledge check 21

How did Newman define 'defensible space'?

Exam tip

In an exam you may need to be able to explain how features of the environment may encourage or deter crime.

Philip Zimbardo (1969) carried out an experiment to test the broken-window theory. Zimbardo arranged for an automobile with no licence plates and the hood up to be parked idle in a Bronx neighbourhood and a second automobile in the same condition to be set up in Palo Alto, California. The car in the Bronx was attacked within minutes of its abandonment and within 24 hours, everything of value had been stripped from the vehicle and after that the car's windows were smashed in, parts torn, upholstery ripped, and children were using the car as a playground. The vehicle in Palo Alto, California, sat untouched until Zimbardo himself went to the vehicle and deliberately smashed it with a sledgehammer. Soon after, people joined in for the destruction. Zimbardo believed that in a neighbourhood such as the Bronx where the history of abandoned property and theft are more prevalent, vandalism occurs much more quickly as the community generally seems apathetic.

Reference: Wilson, J. Q. and Kelling, G. L. (1982) 'The police and neighbourhood safety: broken windows', *Atlantic Monthly*, 127, 29–38

> **Knowledge check 22**
>
> Outline what is meant by 'a zero tolerance policy' to crime.

> **Application**
>
> You must be able to suggest and explain at least one strategy for crime prevention.

Application of broken windows theory

In the mid-1970s the 'Safe and Clean Neighborhoods Program' was designed to improve the quality of community life in 28 USA cities. As part of that programme, money was provided to help cities take police officers out of their patrol cars and assign them to foot patrols. Five years after the programme started, the Police Foundation, in Washington, DC, published an evaluation of the foot-patrol project. The foundation concluded that foot patrol had not reduced crime rates but that residents of the foot-patrolled neighbourhoods tended to believe that crime had been reduced, and seemed to take fewer steps to protect themselves from crime. Also, people in the foot-patrolled areas had a more favourable opinion of the police than did those living elsewhere. Officers walking beats had higher morale, greater job satisfaction, and a more favourable attitude toward people in their neighbourhoods than did officers assigned to patrol cars.

> **Exam tip**
>
> In an exam you may be asked to suggest a strategy to reduce crime, make sure you can apply the broken windows theory.

The urban environment

The physical aspects of a city are presumed to affect residents' behaviour. Details of research on the Pruitt–Igoe urban housing project built in the 1950s are available at www.pruitt-igoe.com/urban-history.

Effect of imprisonment (Social)

You must be able to describe and discuss punishment and reform as responses to criminal behaviour, describe the Haney et al. (1973) study of prisoners and guards in a simulated prison and suggest and explain at least one strategy for reducing reoffending.

Punishment and reform: imprisonment

Farrington et al. (2002)

Many people assume that making prisons stricter will reduce reoffending. However, research does not support this. Farrington et al. (2002) looked at the effect of strict prison conditions in two 'boot camp' regimes. Thorn Cross Training Centre offering a 16 hours a day programme of activities including military drilling and Colchester Young Offender Institution having a programme similar to the Military Corrective Training Centre at Colchester. The expected reconviction rates were compared to actual reconviction rates 2 years after release. In Thorn Cross the experimental group took longer to reoffend and committed significantly fewer crimes, but Farrington concluded that the reduction in reoffending was probably due to the education, employment, mentoring and 'through-care' components rather than to the drilling and physical training.

Risk factors associated with self-harm or suicide in UK prisoners

The Youth Justice Board for England and Wales is an executive non-departmental public body employed to advise the home secretary on the operation of the youth justice system, how to prevent offending by children and young people and to monitor the operation and performance of the youth justice system.

Self-harm within prison

Self-harm is a significant issue for adolescents within prison. **Liebling (1995)** examined factors associated with self-harm in young prisoners. In these studies, it was noted, that all the prisoners had backgrounds with multiple disadvantages. Suicide attempters were more likely to report multiple family breakdown, frequent violence leading to hospitalisation, local authority placement as a result of family breakdown, truancy as a result of bullying, experiences of sexual abuse and previous episodes of self-harm. The suicide attempters found prison life more difficult in most respects. Liebling called this group of young people 'poor copers'.

Suicide within prison

Within prison, 10% of suicides occur within the first 24 hours of imprisonment, 40% within the first month and 80% within the first year. Studies on prison suicide have highlighted the importance of both individual and institutional factors. In studies of completed suicides in England and Wales **(Dooley 1990; HM Chief Inspector of Prisons 1999)** the risk factors identified included mental illness, a history of psychiatric contact (40%), a history of single or multiple substance misuse (30 to 70%), a history of self-harm (50%), loss of social contact and relationship difficulties, victimisation by other inmates and difficulties in coping with the prison regime. Research found that suicide attempters were more likely to have experienced family breakdown or sexual abuse and that a majority of self-inflicted deaths of juveniles occur within the first month of entering custody. The HM Prison Service (2003) surveyed young people and staff in prisons and concluded that the most successful regimes were those where young people received consistent treatment by staff and where staff showed genuine concern or interest in prisoners' welfare and progress.

Institutional aggression in the context of prisons

In 2006, across England and Wales, there were 11,476 violent incidents between prisoners. This shows that prisons can be violent places for both prisoners and staff.

Why interpersonal violence occurs in prisons

Two major models (theories) have been proposed in an attempt to understand why interpersonal violence occurs frequently in prisons — the dispositional explanation (the importation model) and the situational explanation (the deprivation model).

The dispositional explanation: the importation model

This explanation suggests that offenders enter prison with particular characteristics, such as personality traits, values and attitudes and that these characteristics (dispositional factors) predict they are more likely to engage in interpersonal aggression. According to the dispositional theory, aggression is not a product of the institution but is caused by the characteristics of the individual.

Research evidence

- Adams (1981) found that younger inmates are thought to have a more difficult time than older inmates when adjusting to prison life, as a result, they are more likely to have confrontations with other inmates and staff and view violence as appropriate during conflict.
- Keller and Wang (2005) found that prison violence is more likely to occur in facilities that hold troublesome inmates. For example, prisons holding maximum-security inmates had higher levels of violence.
- Harer and Steffensmeier (1996) analysed data from 58 male US prisons and found that black inmates displayed higher levels of violent behaviour compared to white inmates. They concluded that the black offenders often entered prison from impoverished communities with higher levels of violent crimes and so they bring into the prison the cultural norms which condone violence.

Evaluation

- **McCorkle et al. (1995)** claimed that the model fails to provide suggestions for how best to manage violent behaviour or how to reduce it in general.
- A limitation of the dispositional explanation is the suggestion that aggression is caused by nature rather than nurture, it ignores the environmental situation of the inmates and is thus a reductionist explanation.
- A limitation of research into institutional aggression within prisons is that there is a gender bias as it is only the behaviour of men which is analysed and therefore researchers take an androcentric (male based) view of aggression.

The situational explanation: the deprivation model

The situational explanation (the deprivation model) suggests that it is the situational factors of the prison that account for aggression and that the experience of imprisonment causes inmates stress and frustration, which leads to aggression and violence. For example, the overcrowding crisis in UK prisons forces many inmates to share cells, which is linked to an increase in interpersonal violence, self-harm and suicide. **Harer and Steffensmeier (1996)** suggest that an inmate's aggressive behaviour is a response to the problems and frustrations of adjusting to loss of freedom and to the isolation, boredom and loneliness of being in prison.

Key research

Haney et al. (1973) 'Study of prisoners and guards in a simulated prison'

In the **Stanford Prison Experiment** 24 young, educated, male participants were assigned to the role of either a prisoner or prison guard in a mock prison. The study had to be stopped on day 6 because the guards lost their normal sense of identity and behaved appallingly towards the prisoners, humiliating them both emotionally and physically. All the participants had been tested for mental health prior to the experiment and no abnormal or aggressive traits were found prior to the study taking place.

Within 48 hours prisoners became anxious and depressed and Zimbardo suggested they suffered from deindividuation and learned helplessness. Zimbardo suggested that the students who played the role of guards became brutal and abusive towards the prisoners because peer pressure led to the guards' brutality, and that people are more likely to be aggressive when they dehumanise others in an institution without 'external restraint'.

The conclusion was that people will readily conform to the social roles they are expected to play, especially if the roles are as strongly stereotyped as those of the prison guards. The 'prison' environment was an important factor in creating the guards' brutal behaviour. The findings support the situational explanation of behaviour rather than the dispositional one.

Reference: Haney, C., Banks, W. C. and Zimbardo, P. G. (1973) 'Study of prisoners and guards in a simulated prison', *Naval Research Reviews*, 9, 1–17

Evaluation

- Zimbardo's explanation of institutional aggression is useful as it has real-life relevance. **Zimbardo (2007)** claims that the same social psychological processes found in the Stanford Prison Experiment were also apparent during the abuse of Iraqi prisoners at Abu Ghraib prison in Iraq. These included deindividuation and dehumanisation which led to a lack of accountability for the brutal actions towards the 'prisoners'.

Knowledge check 23

Thinking about aggressive behaviour in prison, explain the difference between the importation model and the deprivation model.

Exam tip

Prepare to apply the debate concerning the 'individual vs situational' explanation of behaviour to a discussion of institutional violence.

- **McCorkle et al. (1995)** suggest that the levels of stress associated with imprisonment are constant, whereas outbreaks of violence are not. They claim violence is due to the management of prisons. They studied 371 state prisons in the USA and found little evidence to support the connection between violence and environmental factors such as overcrowding and living conditions.
- **Reicher and Haslam (2006)** argue that institutional aggression in prisons is more to do with one group's way of thinking about the other group. For example, in the Second World War, German captors treated their prisoners differently — British prisoners were considered equal and treated in a civilised manor, whereas Russian prisoners were seen as subhuman and treated barbarically.
- Research by both Zimbardo and Bandura is unethical and because all participants were students, the samples are not representative and cannot be generalised to the population of offenders in prisons.

> **Exam tip**
>
> You need to be able to explain why it is difficult to 'prove' whether dispositional factors or situational factors cause aggressive behaviour in prisons.

Application

You must be able to apply the research you have learned to suggest and explain at least one strategy for reducing reoffending.

Punishment and reform: community sentences

'Punishment and reform: effective community sentences' was presented to Parliament by the lord chancellor and secretary of state for justice in October 2012. (It is available for download at www.official-documents.gov.uk and at www.justice.gov.uk.)

The lord chancellor's report suggests that prisons do too little to challenge the individuals who end up inside them and nearly half those leaving prison reoffend within a year. The report also suggests that reoffending rates for community sentences remain too high and community sentences lack credibility as effective punishment. The report recommends stronger community sentences to rehabilitate and reduce crime. The suggestions include:

- Community sentences to be extended from 6 to 12 months to involve a full 5-day week of hard work and job seeking.
- The courts should be able to access data held by the taxman so offenders cannot hide their true incomes.
- Using new technology, location monitoring will ensure that offenders can be found and that there are always consequences for offenders who breach the terms of their sentences.
- Restorative justice (RJ) should be used across the justice system.
- Electronic monitoring and curfews should be used to prevent offenders from being in places that may increase their risk of offending.

> **Exam tip**
>
> Make sure you can explain why it is difficult to obtain a valid measurement of the effectiveness of punishment.

Summary

You should be able to:
- describe concepts, theories and studies specified by the indicative content:
  - what makes a criminal
  - collection and processing of forensic evidence
  - collection of evidence from witnesses and suspects
  - psychology and the courtroom
  - crime prevention
  - effect of imprisonment
- apply the methodological issues and debates in psychology
- recognise the contribution key research has made to the topic
- apply the background, research and application to novel situations
- consider how different areas of psychology can inform our understanding of applied psychology
- explore social, moral, cultural and spiritual issues where applicable
- recognise how research contributes to an understanding of individual, social and cultural diversity
- recognise how society makes decisions about scientific issues and how psychology is useful in society

When answering questions on applied psychology you will be expected to illustrate your answers with knowledge and understanding of the issues and debates in psychology.

■ Environmental psychology

This section looks at how psychology can be applied to the topics — stressors in the environment, biological rhythms and the impact of their disruption on behaviour, recycling and conservation behaviours, ergonomics, the effects of the built environment and territory and personal space. For each of these topics you must learn some background theories, key research evidence, and how the topic can be applied to environmental psychology. For these topics you should also be able to discuss and apply psychological research methods, perspectives, issues and debates. You also need to be able to answer questions such as 'Assess the extent to which individual or situational factors explain recycling and other conservation behaviours'.

Stressors in the environment (Biological)

Stress is a type of alarm reaction, involving heightened mental and bodily states. It is both a physiological and psychological response to the environment. Thus, stress can be defined as the response that happens when we think we cannot cope with a stressor in the environment. If we think we cannot cope, we feel stress, and when we feel stress, we experience physiological changes.

The physiology of stress

Physiological explanations of stress focus on how and why the brain and nervous system respond to stressors, for example, the role of the **autonomic nervous system** and the **pituitary-adrenal system** and the effect of stress on the **immune system**.

Selye (1956) proposed that stress leads to a depletion of the body's resources, leaving the animal vulnerable to illness. He used the word 'stress' to describe the fact that many different stimuli (e.g. fear, pain, injury) all produce the same response. He called these 'stressors' and proposed that the body reacts in the same general way to all these stressors by producing a response which helps the animal adapt to them and continue to function. Selye defined two types of stress — eustress (good stress) and distress (bad stress). Both eustress and distress release the stress hormone cortisol. During **distress** when cortisol is released your body becomes mobilised and ready for 'fight or flight' and unless there is some physical action (e.g. you run away from the snarling dog) cortisol levels build up in the blood which presents risk to health. In comparison, during **eustress** there is a heightened state of arousal and cortisol levels return to normal on completion of the task.

The hypothalamic-pituitary-adrenal system (HPA)

The hypothalamic-pituitary-adrenal system (HPA) is activated by chronic stress (e.g. worry about the illness of a family member or even about exams). The stress response originates in the hypothalamus and includes the pituitary and adrenal glands. This hypothalamic-pituitary-adrenal axis is responsible for arousing the autonomic nervous system (ANS) in response to a stressor. Under stress, the sympathetic branch of the nervous system stimulates the adrenal gland to release adrenaline, noradrenaline and corticosteroids into the bloodstream. This produces the physiological reactions, such as increased heart rate and blood pressure and a dry mouth, known as the 'fight-or-flight' response.

The stress hormone cortisol

The stress hormone cortisol can cause damage to health because raised cortisol levels lower immune function and bone density and also increase the risk of depression and mental illness. High cortisol levels have been found to be a potential trigger for mental illness, especially in adolescence. Cortisol is released in response to fear or stress by the adrenal glands as part of the fight-or-flight mechanism.

Stress and the immune system

The immune system comprises billions of cells produced in the bone marrow, spleen, lymph nodes and thymus. The major type of immune cell is the white blood cell, which defends the body against bacteria, viruses and cancerous cells. When we are stressed, the ability of the immune system to protect us is reduced, leading to an increased likelihood of physical illness. This weakening of the immune system is called the **immune-suppressive effect of stress**.

Stress and cardiovascular disorders

Long-term stress may also have a direct effect on the cardiovascular system. Stress causes high heart rate and high blood pressure. Long-term stress can damage blood vessels because adrenaline and noradrenaline contribute to increases in blood cholesterol levels, leading to blood clots and thickened arteries. Weakened or damaged blood vessels may cause haemorrhages, which in turn may lead to blockages in blood vessels, causing strokes or heart attacks.

Sources of stress

Workplace stress: workload and control

Stress in the workplace can originate in **six areas**:

(1) **Interpersonal factors.** Relationships with bosses, colleagues and customers may be stressful. Social support is important in moderating the effects of stress in

Knowledge check 24

When we are in a stressful situation what causes the 'flight-or-fight' response symptoms such as increased heart rate and blood pressure and a dry mouth?

Knowledge check 25

Outline how stress affects the immune system.

general. Good relationships with co-workers can reduce stress in the workplace; poor relationships at work can exacerbate stress.

(2) **Workload and pressure.** Having too much work to do and working to strict deadlines can cause stress.

(3) **The physical environment.** This may be noisy, hot and overcrowded, or may involve health risks and unsociable hours, such as working night shifts. Czeisler et al. (1982) researched the causes of health problems and sleep difficulties experienced by employees of a chemical plant in Utah, USA. The employees worked shifts. Czeisler recommended that the pattern of shifts should be changed to a 21-day shift rotation and always 'shift forward' (phase advance). After 9 months, job satisfaction and productivity increased.

(4) **Role stress.** Worry about job security or responsibility may cause stress.

(5) **Role conflict.** Having to express one emotion while feeling another may cause stress (e.g. in doctors, nurses, police).

(6) **Control.** How much control people have over how they do a job may be a factor in how stressful the job is perceived to be.

Environmental stressors and their effects

Light

Seasonal changes in light may cause Seasonal Affective Disorder (SAD) in some people. SAD is thought to be caused by lack of light in winter when days are shorter. The main biological effect of lack of light may be on the production of melatonin by the pineal gland. Melatonin is a substance that affects mood and energy levels.

Temperature

Psychologists propose that hot weather is a factor in the increase of stress-related aggressive behaviour. Baron and Bell (1976) propose that negative moods and aggression increase when weather becomes uncomfortably hot, and that if escape from the heat is not possible aggressive behaviour is likely. Kenrick and MacFarlane (1986) observed the behaviour of drivers at traffic lights in hot weather. They recorded the number of times other drivers hooted at them when although the traffic lights turned green their car remained stationary. The **'negative effect escape theory'** of Baron and Bell would explain this. The hooting drivers were trapped in their overheated cars and the stationary car was blocking the escape. Anderson (1987) analysed data for crimes such as murder, rape, assault, burglaries and car theft and found that the rate of violent crimes (e.g. murder, rape, assault) increased in the hot parts of years and that there was a positive correlation between temperature and violent crime.

There may be a biological explanation as to why aggressive behaviour increases in hot weather. Research shows that the hormone testosterone is related to increases in aggressive behaviour. Testosterone is a male hormone, which may explain why males are more aggressive than females. In hot weather the autonomic nervous system is activated and the adrenal cortex produces corticosteroids, which increase the production of testosterone (Anderson and Anderson 1998).

Barometric pressure and air pollution

A stressful weather pattern is associated with warm, low pressure weather. Wind that is warm and dry is associated with high levels of positive ions and with an increase in depression and irritability. Rotton and Frey (1984) reported an increase in psychiatric emergencies on days when carbon monoxide, ozone and nitrogen dioxide pollution was higher.

Noise

Noise is measured on a decibel (dB) scale. The threshold for hearing is 0 dB. Normal conversation is about 40 dB, while the noise around a busy street is about 70 dB, and a rock band might be 120 dB. Long exposure to 90 dB can damage the eardrums. Sudden and unexpected noise produces increased blood pressure and increased heart rate, but these changes wear off as people become accustomed to the noise (Broadbent 1957). However, even when a person is accustomed to an environment in which noise level is high, physiological and psychological changes occur and people express dislike of being disturbed by noise. A study reported by Cohen and his colleagues (1986) found that children living on the lower floors of a particular high-rise apartment building had poorer hearing abilities and more problems with reading than did children on the upper floors. The apartment building was built near a freeway and the noise levels were blamed for the deficiencies of the children living on the lower floors.

Crowding

Being in a crowd may be related to increases in aggressive behaviour due to 'crowding'. Crowding is a subjective psychological experience that will vary between individuals. A famous study of crowding involved rats. Calhoun (1962) studied rats allowed to breed in a restricted space. The dominant rats took up most of the space and the less dominant rats were crowded into what Calhoun called ' a behavioural sink' in which aggressive behaviour was high, nest building and offspring care decreased, and killing and even cannibalising each other was common. Psychologists have also found that crowding in humans is associated with increases in aggression. Cox et al. (1984) reported a positive correlation between aggression and crowding in a prison, where a 30% reduction in the prison population led to a 60% reduction in assaults on other inmates.

> **Knowledge check 26**
>
> List three environmental stressors.

> **Exam tip**
>
> Referring to situational vs dispositional causes of behaviour it would be useful if you can explain one weakness of the suggestion that crowding causes aggressive behaviour.

Key research

Black, D. A. and Black, J. A. (2007) 'Aircraft noise exposure and residents' stress and hypertension'

Aim: A cross-sectional study of environmental noise and community health was conducted in residential neighbourhoods near Sydney airport with high exposure to aircraft noise and in a matched control suburb unaffected by aircraft noise.

Participants: Suburbs around the flight path of Sydney airport were selected for the aircraft noise exposure area, due to having more than 50 events of aircraft noise louder than 70 dB per day; 750 subjects were sent a survey.

Control areas: locations not exposed to aircraft matched on socioeconomic status to exposure area; 750 subjects were sent a survey.

Procedure: Field data: noise stations were set up outside randomly selected households: 26 located around Sydney airport and three in the control area from 7 a.m. to 6 p.m., October to November. A night-time curfew of flights was imposed between 11 p.m. and 6 a.m.

Survey data: Subjective health outcomes were measured by a questionnaire. Subjects were sent a cover letter detailing the study was on environmental noise (omitting mention of aircraft noise specifically). The questionnaire measured seven major characteristics:

1   Health-related quality of life

2   Hypertension condition — assessed by closed questions, e.g. 'Have you ever been told by a doctor that you have high blood pressure?' YES/NO

3   Noise stress

4   Noise sensitivity

5   Noise annoyance

6   Demographic characteristics

7   Confounding factors such as exercise, smoking status etc.

Results: People in the noise exposure group were more sharply annoyed by aircraft noise than controls. While hypertension was slightly higher in the controls than the noise exposure group, this was not significant. Those in the noise exposure group did however show a less positive health status compared to controls, notably with mental health ($p \leftarrow 0.001$).

Conclusions: The mean score of physical functioning, general health, vitality and mental health of the noise exposure group was significantly lower than the matched control implying that noise exposure from the airport's flight path did have an impact on general health. Long-term aircraft noise exposure was significantly associated with chronic noise stress (odds of 2.61) and this was thus associated with the prevalence of hypertension (odds of 2.74) compared to those without chronic noise stress. It was concluded that people who have been chronically exposed to high aircraft noise level are more likely to report stress and hypertension compared with those not exposed to aircraft noise.

Reference: Black, D. A. and Black, J. A. (2007) 'Aircraft noise exposure and residents' stress and hypertension: a public health perspective for airport environmental management', *Journal of Air Transport Management* 13 (5), 264–76

> **Knowledge check 27**
>
> Suggest one strength and one weakness of the Black and Black research into the effect of aircraft noise.

Application

You must be able to apply the research you have learned to suggest and explain at least one strategy for managing environmental stress.

Applied research: treating SAD

The symptoms of SAD can be reduced by sitting patients in front of very bright artificial lights for at least 1 hour per day. This lowers the levels of melatonin in the bloodstream which in turn reduces the feelings of depression. Terman et al. (1998)

researched 124 participants with SAD: 85 were given a 30-minute exposure to bright light, some in the morning, and some in the evening; another 39 were exposed to negative ions (a placebo group). Of the morning bright light group 60% showed significant improvement compared to only 30% of those getting light in the evening. Only 5% of the placebo group showed improvement. The researchers concluded that bright light may be acting as a zeitgeber to reset the body clock in the morning.

Exam tip

You must be able to suggest a strategy to help people who live in a city cope with one environmental stressor.

Biological rhythms (Biological)

This topic looks at biological rhythms and the impact of their disruption on our behaviour. The key research is by Czeisler et al. (1982), a study showing that rotating shift work schedules that disrupt sleep are improved by applying circadian principles. You should be able to apply this and other research to suggest and explain at least one strategy for reducing the effects of jetlag or shift work.

Biological rhythms and the impact of their disruption on behaviour

Circadian rhythms

The word 'circadian' stems from the Latin — *circa* (meaning 'about') and *diem* (meaning 'day'). There are some cycles that we are consciously aware of — the sleep/wake cycle being an obvious one. But there are other cycles we are not aware of, for example, our body temperature fluctuates over a 24-hour period. Generally it peaks mid-afternoon at about 37.1 °C and troughs in the small hours at about 36.7 °C.

Biological basis of circadian rhythms

In non-human species, the pineal gland appears to be the brain structure responsible for regulating the circadian sleep/wake cycle. In humans, the suprachiasmatic nucleus (SCN) appears to control the sleep/wake cycle. The SCN is situated in the hypothalamus just behind the eyes and receives sensory input about light levels through the optic nerve. The SCN appears to be the location of the main 'body clock'.

Internal (endogenous) pacemakers

To study endogenous pacemakers it is necessary to isolate people from external cues for many months. Over the past 40 years, French geologist Michael Siffre has regularly spent extended periods of time in various caves around the world and has been studied during the process. In 1962 he spent 61 days in a cave in the Alps. He emerged in September but thought it was August and had lost 28 days. In 1972 he was monitored in the caves of Texas. Each time his body clock extended from the usual 24 to around 24.5 hours which appears to suggest:

- There is internal control (endogenous) of the circadian rhythm because even in the absence of external cues we are able to maintain a regular daily cycle.
- There must usually be some external cue that keeps this cycle to 24 hours because when this is removed we adopt a 24.5 or 25-hour cycle.

External pacemakers (exogenous zeitgebers)

Light appears to be crucial in maintaining the 24-hour circadian rhythm. Campbell and Murphy (1998) shone bright lights onto the back of participants' knees and were able to alter their circadian rhythms in line with the light exposure. The exact mechanism for this is unclear, but it seems possible that the blood chemistry was altered and this was detected by the SCN. Miles et al. (1977) reported the case study of a blind man who had a daily rhythm of 24.9 hours. Zeitgebers such as clocks or radios failed to reset the endogenous clock and the man relied on stimulants and sedatives to maintain a 24-hour sleep/wake cycle. Luce and Segal (1966) found that on the Arctic Circle people maintain a reasonably constant sleep pattern, averaging 7 hours a night, despite 6 months of darkness in the winter months, followed by 6 months of light in the summer. In these conditions it seems that social factors reset endogenous rhythms rather than light levels.

Infradian rhythms

Infradian rhythms occur over a period of time greater than 24 hours. In humans the best examples are the menstrual cycle and PMS (pre-menstrual syndrome) which occurs a few days prior to the onset of bleeding and is characterised by loss of appetite, stress, irritability and poor concentration. There are a number of rhythms that are cyclic over about 1 year. Examples include migration, mating patterns and hibernation in the animal world and SAD (Seasonal Affective Disorder) in humans. The symptoms of SAD can be reduced by sitting patients in front of very bright artificial lights for at least 1 hour per day. This lowers the levels of melatonin in the bloodstream which in turn reduces the feelings of depression. The researchers concluded that bright light administered in this way may be acting as a zeitgeber and resetting the body clock in the morning.

Ultradian rhythms

An ultradian rhythm is one that repeats itself over a period of less than 24 hours. Ultradian rhythms occur more than once in a 24-hour cycle and most are confined to either day or night. Sleep is an example of an ultradian rhythm as the cycle of sleep typically lasts about 90 minutes and during a typical night of sleep we will repeat this cycle four or five times. The stages of sleep can be monitored using EEG. REM sleep (rapid eye movement) is strange because the brain becomes very active, almost like a waking brain. Heart rate and blood pressure increase and the eyes move rapidly giving this stage its name. Our first REM sleep lasts for about 10 minutes and then we start our journey back down to stage 2, stage 3 and stage 4 sleep. This cycle repeats throughout the night. There are large individual differences between people and some may sleep for much shorter periods, but others who have been sleep deprived will spend longer in stage 4 and REM sleep.

Jetlag and shift work

In normal circumstances our biological body clocks are not in conflict with external zeitgebers. The daily pattern of life, waking in the morning at or around sunrise, working through the day when our metabolism and body temperature are at their peak and going to sleep at night when it gets dark, causes no disruption. However, there are situations now when our internal clocks do come into conflict with external cues, such as dark/light. The two obvious examples are shift work when we operate on a rotating schedule of hours and jet lag when we travel across time zones either east to west or west to east.

Knowledge check 28

State the difference between circadian, infradian and ultradian rhythms.

Exam tip

In the exam you may need to be able to give an example of a biological rhythm.

Jetlag

Jetlag or desynchronosis is caused by the body's internal body clock being out of step with external cues. This results in a number of symptoms including fatigue, insomnia, anxiety, dehydration and increased susceptibility to illness.

- **Phase advance:** getting up or going to bed earlier than usual (flying W to E)
- **Phase delay:** getting up or going to bed later than usual (flying E to W)

In general it is easier to adjust to phase delay. Possibly because phase delay is effectively lengthening our day and our internal rhythm is greater than 24 hours. Phase delay therefore brings external factors closer in line with internal ones whereas phase advance moves them further away.

Shift work

Other species abide by natural laws and are governed by their inbuilt biological rhythms. It is only humans with their 24-hour lifestyle who suffer desycnchronisation due to working against biorhythms. In the industrialised world 20% of workers work some form of rotating or permanent unsocial shift pattern. Shift work results in fatigue, sleep disturbance, digestive problems, lack of concentration, memory loss and mood swings.

Shift work is usually more troublesome than jet lag since it involves prolonged conflict between internal clocks and external stimuli. This situation is often compounded by:

- the person reverting to 'normal' sleep/wake cycles at the weekend
- shifts altering from one week to the next

As a result, people never adapt to a new rhythm, leaving their biorhythms in a permanent state of desynchronisation. This can result in reduced productivity. There are also health risks associated with regular shift work. These include an increased risk of heart disease and digestive disorders and regular tiredness — 20% of shift workers report falling asleep while at work. Shifts can follow a number of patterns.

Rotating or fixed shifts

Fixed shifts tend to be rare, mostly because of the unsociable hours involved (e.g. working a permanent 10 p.m. to 6 a.m. shift). Although this allows time for resynchronisation with the worker adjusting to the shift pattern it does create problems at weekends when people revert back to a normal sleep-wake pattern. A rotating pattern involves working different hours each week or month. A typical three shift system covering a 24 hour period would involve people working:

- 6 a.m. to 2 p.m.
- 2 p.m. to 10 p.m.
- 10 p.m. to 6 a.m.

Cooper et al. (2005) compared rotating shift patterns with fixed shifts. Oil rig workers on either 12-hour day shifts or 12-hour night shifts were compared to workers on a split-shift pattern (working 7 days of night shifts followed by 7 days of day shifts). Urine tests measuring melatonin levels showed that those on split shifts never fully synchronised. They also had significantly higher levels of circulating fatty acids putting them at greater risk of CHD and hypertension.

Clockwise or anticlockwise shift rotation

Shift rotation can be clockwise or anticlockwise. In the example above, week 1 would be 6 a.m. to 2 p.m. in the first week and the 2 p.m. to 10 p.m. shift in week 2 and so on. This is clockwise. A backward (or anticlockwise) rotation would involve starting at 6 a.m. to 2 p.m. in week 1 and then moving to 10 p.m. to 6 a.m. in week 2 and so on. A rotating shift pattern can lead to permanent desynchronisation between internal and external factors and the person may never fully adjust to the new shift.

Fast or slow rotation

Most research suggests a clockwise rotation is to be preferred, but there is disagreement over the speed of rotation. Czeisler recommends a slow rotation, for example spending at least 3 weeks on each shift. Bambra (2008) however, prefers a faster rotation of just 3 to 4 days on each pattern so the body never has time to adjust to the new cycle.

> **Exam tip**
>
> Be prepared to explain how and why shift work disrupts biological rhythms.

Key research

Czeisler et al. (1982) 'Rotating shift work schedules that disrupt sleep are improved by applying circadian principles'

Method/Design: Field experiment using a matched groups design with comparable jobs.

Participants: 85 male rotating shift workers, aged 19–68 (mean 31.4). Control group of 68 male non-rotating day and swing shift workers with comparable jobs aged 19–56 (mean 27.3). All participants selected from the Great Salt Lake Minerals and Chemicals corporation in Utah.

Procedure:

- 33 rotating shift workers on **phase advance shifts** (nights, afternoons and then mornings) rotated 8-hour shifts **every 7 days**. These continuing on their normal work shifts: Shift 1: 12 a.m. – 8 a.m.; Shift 2: 4 p.m. – 12 a.m.; Shift 3: 8 a.m. – 4 p.m.
- 52 shift workers by **phase delay** (nights, then mornings, then afternoons) rotated shifts but changing once **every 21 days**.
- Each worker was given self-reports on health measures, sleepiness and schedule preference. Staff turnover and plant productivity (potash production) were analysed 9 months after implementing the new schedules.

Results:

- The response rate was 84%.
- Rotating shift workers reported significantly more problems with insomnia than the non-rotators — 29% rotators reported falling asleep at work at least once in past 3 months.
- Workers clearly preferred phase delay shift, with complaints of schedule dropping from 90 to 20% among those on the phase delay shift. This was associated with a reduction of staff turnover and increase in productivity.

→

Conclusions: Work schedules that rotate by phase delay with an extended interval between each rotation are most compatible with the properties of the human circadian rhythm. However, any new schedule must take into consideration the nature of work and the needs of workers.

Reference: Czeisler, C. A., Moore-Ede, M. C. and Coleman, R. M. (1982) 'Rotating shift work schedules that disrupt sleep are improved by applying circadian principles', *Science*, 217, 460–63

Knowledge check 29

Summarise what Czeisler (1982) recommended for shift workers.

Application

You must be able to apply the research you have learned to suggest and explain at least one strategy for reducing the effects of jetlag or shift work.

Using artificial light to reset the body clock

Boivin et al. (1996) studied 31 male participants who were awake at night and sleeping during the day for 3 days. Each day when they woke they sat in front of dim lights for 5 hours and were then placed in one of four conditions: very bright light; bright light; ordinary room light; continued dim light. Core body temperature was recorded and used as a measure of how well they were adapting to the new rhythm. After 3 days:

- Group 1 had advanced by 5 hours (they were adapting to the new pattern best)
- Group 2 had advanced by 3 hours
- Group 3 had advanced by 1 hour
- Group 4 had drifted backwards by 1 hour (they were failing to show any signs of adapting)

They concluded that artificial light, even ordinary room light can help us adapt our biological rhythms to suit the environment, but brighter light is even more effective. This could be useful in the workplace to help shift workers to adapt to changing sleep-wake cycles.

Using melatonin to reset the body clock

Melatonin is the chemical secreted at night. It enables us to switch off the RAS (that keeps us awake during the day). Taken just prior to bedtime in the new time zone, melatonin has been shown to be effective in allowing sufferers of jet lag to get to sleep sooner than their body clock would normally allow. Melatonin is used by US military pilots to adapt to differing time zones.

Note: see also the section on Seasonal Affective Disorder on p. 49.

Exam tip

You must be able to make a suggestion as to what pattern of shift work is best for productivity and employee health.

Recycling and other conservation behaviours (Cognitive)

This topic looks at conservation behaviours and the factors which influence the tendency to conserve or recycle. The key research is Lord (1994) 'Motivating recycling behaviour — a quasi-experimental investigation of message and source strategies'.

You should be able to apply this and other research to suggest and explain at least one strategy for increasing recycling or other conservation behaviour.

Factors which influence the tendency to conserve or recycle

Persuasive messages

We all know we should recycle but often do not bother to put our plastic, paper, glass and metal into the right bin(s). Research suggests that using the 'right kind of message' encourages people to recycle. There are two kinds of message — those that **highlight the negative consequences** of not recycling (loss) and those that **emphasise the positive consequences** of recycling (gain). Which is most effective?

Research suggests that it depends on whether you want people to focus on concrete details like when to put the recycling bin out, or abstract ideas about why recycling is important. Researchers prepared different door hangers about recycling — some with loss and some with gain messages. On the reverse side of some, they listed concrete steps for how to recycle, including specifics about the type of items and the time and place to put the material for collection. On the reverse side of others, they asked people to think more abstractly about why recycling contributed to the community, air, land and water resources. When the actual quantities of material recycled were monitored, researchers found that negative information (loss) worked best to get people to recycle when paired with concrete instructions about how to recycle. Positive information (gain) about what recycling accomplishes also worked when it was matched with statements about why recycling is important. In other words, if you are going to give people bad news to motivate them, it is best to give them information about what to do. Otherwise, focus on good news and pair it with information on why the action is important. Least effective is matching a negative message with abstract reasons for recycling, or pairing a positive but abstract message with concrete information.

Extrinsic or intrinsic motivation

Much research into the encouragement to recycle has applied behaviourist theories and research on recycling programmes has emphasised the use of extrinsic incentives and positive reinforcement strategies. There are a number of behaviourist strategies that are effective at motivating recycling.

Extrinsic motivation

Raffle tickets, coupons and eligibility for lottery prizes have been used as positive reinforcement for participation in residential recycling programmes (Jacobs and Bailey 1982–83). However, once the incentives are taken away, the behaviour often stops, perhaps because people come to believe that the reason they are recycling is for the reward, so when the reward is withdrawn the recycling stops. Also, using rewards to increase recycling may be impractical since the cost of the incentives may prevent recycling programmes from being cost-effective. Incentives that are external to the individual (e.g. money, food or prizes) should not be too large because a small reward that promotes self-determination may increase intrinsic motivation. Pro-social rewards, such as a donation to charity, may be effective because these reward

> **Knowledge check 30**
>
> 'Forests are disappearing so please put all your used paper and board into the recycling bin.' Explain whether this message is likely to persuade people to recycle.

participants for doing the 'right behaviour' while also making them feel they are 'good people' so a pro-social reward can prevent a decrease in intrinsic motivation.

Intrinsic motivation

Much human behaviour is explained in terms of the intrinsic reward that arises out of participation in an ongoing activity. In a study of newspaper recycling, participants were asked either to give a verbal commitment to recycle or to sign a legally non-binding commitment statement and were found to maintain recycling behaviour. These participants were committed to carry out the behaviour and so may have found their own reasons for recycling, enjoyed doing so, and thus continued to recycle.

Positive emotional states

Appealing to positive emotional states may be more effective than appealing to negative emotions because positive messages tend to be perceived as more credible, and result in people being more open to new thoughts and behaviours. In a study on recycling, respondents indicated that they preferred rewards to penalties, and that being penalised for not recycling did not cause them to take recycling more seriously. Using fear tactics or punishment such as fines, or 'doom' messages about negative environmental futures can lead to scepticism, feelings of helplessness and decreased intention to act. Negative emotions have been shown to lead to short-term thinking and less ability to plan for the future. Positive messages or positive feedback may result in feelings of accomplishment that encourage continued recycling behaviour.

> **Exam tip**
>
> Be prepared to suggest one method that can be used to encourage people to recycle.

Social norms

Social psychologists have studied the effects of social norms on behaviour and the idea that to produce a lasting change in behaviour, it is important to change the social context (Lewin 1947). Also, attitude-behaviour correspondence is increased by attending to the role of social norms in behaviour. In regards to recycling, McGuinness, Jones and Cole (1977) found perceived social support for recycling was related to recycling behaviour.

Research evidence

Burn, S. (2006) found that personal contact with individuals within a neighbourhood is the most effective way to increase recycling within a community. In this study 10 block leaders talked to their neighbours and persuaded them to recycle. A comparison group was sent fliers promoting recycling. It was found that the neighbours who were personally contacted by their block leaders recycled much more than the group without personal contact. This study showed that a personal contact within a small group of people is an important factor in encouraging recycling.

Key research

Lord, K. R. (1994) 'Motivating recycling behaviour: a quasi-experimental investigation of message and source strategies'

Method/Design: Quasi-experimental method using direct behavioural observations and survey data. Independent groups design used where each household was allocated to one of three conditions for message source and one of two for message framing.

Participants and sampling: 140 households were used to collect data in a northeastern community in New York State. Quota sampling was used to ensure the representation of multiple neighbourhoods and diverse socioeconomic characteristics — 57% of respondents were female, aged 19–65.

Procedure: Students observed and recorded the contents of each household's recycling bin. The following day, they left a message (different conditions below) at the front door. The following week, observation took place again. The day after, a questionnaire was delivered to each household asking subjects to evaluate the truthfulness of certain statements about recycling behaviour with a 7-point scale. It also made use of semantic differential scales to measure attitudes towards recycling. Message sources: advertisement, newspaper article, personal letter from acquaintance. Message framing: positive — environmental benefits, savings to community and person satisfaction; negative — described risks of failing to recycle.

Results: Positive appeals gave the most favourable levels of beliefs towards recycling, particularly when combined with personal and advertising message sources. The greatest increase in recycling behaviour came from the negatively framed message when presented by a personal acquaintance.

Conclusions: Consumer response to appeals to increase compliance to community recycling programmes is complex. Consumers have a preference for positively framed messages with the advantage that it is more believable. The credibility advantage of news organisations is that when presenting a negatively framed message it enhances the believability of its claims and overcomes any adverse effects. The use of advertising space to promote socially responsible behaviour rather than a product gives it more credibility. The obvious advantages of recycling are the long-term environmental benefits so personal consequences will have less impact.

Reference: Lord, K. R. (1994) 'Motivating recycling behaviour: a quasi-experimental investigation of message and source strategies', *Psychology and Marketing*, 11 (4), 341–58

Knowledge check 31

Summarise the findings of the Lord (1994) research into motivating recycling behaviour.

Application

You must be able to apply the research you have learned to suggest and explain at least one technique used to increase recycling or other conservation behaviour. You should be able to suggest what sort of message might persuade people to recycle, whether to use extrinsic or intrinsic motivation and how social psychology can be applied to encourage recycling.

Exam tip

Be ready to suggest and explain one strategy to increase recycling behaviour.

Ergonomics: human factors (Cognitive)

Cognitive overload and the impact of observation in the workplace environment

This section looks at two topics, cognitive overload and the impact of observation in the workplace environment. The key research is by Drews and Doig (2014) who evaluated a configural vital sign display for intensive care unit nurses. You must be able to describe and evaluate research into these areas and be ready to suggest and explain at least one workplace design based on ergonomic research.

Cognitive overload

Today's workplace is a complex environment. People struggle to manage and process information effectively in a workspace saturated with multi-tasking, interruption and information overload. The effect of this cognitive overload may be tension with colleagues, loss of job satisfaction and strained personal relationships.

In cognitive psychology, **cognitive load** refers to the total amount of mental effort being used in the working memory. Cognitive load theory categorises cognitive load into three types:

- Intrinsic cognitive load is the effort associated with a specific topic.
- Extraneous cognitive load refers to the way information or tasks are presented.
- Germane cognitive load refers to the work put into creating a permanent store of knowledge.

Heavy cognitive load can have negative effects on task completion.

Cognitive load theory suggests that people can absorb and retain information effectively only if it is provided in such a way that it does not overload their mental capacity. In other words, our **short-term memory**, or **working memory**, can only retain a certain amount of information simultaneously. The more information that is delivered at once the less likely it is to be remembered for later use.

Reminder: 'chunking' information in different ways can reduce cognitive overload.

Short-term memory and long-term memory

Psychologists distinguish between **short-term memory** (STM) and **long-term memory** (LTM). STM cannot hold much information and has limited capacity, whereas LTM can hold an apparently unlimited amount of information and has a vast capacity. George Miller theorised that the capacity of STM is approximately 'seven plus or minus two' pieces of information, but that this capacity can be extended by chunking, or combining, small pieces of information.

The multi-store model of memory (Atkinson and Shiffrin 1968)

Models, or theories, of memory aim to explain how information is transferred from STM to LTM, and why sometimes it is not. In their **multi-store model of memory**, Atkinson and Shiffrin suggest that memory comprises three separate stores: the sensory memory store, the STM and the LTM. Each store has a specific function, as shown in Figure 1.

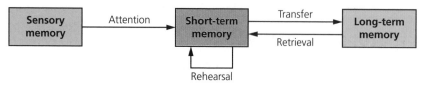

Figure 1 Multi-store model

In the multi-store model, information is rehearsed in STM and, if rehearsed enough, is transferred to LTM. There are three stages of information processing in the multi-store model of memory:

- Stage 1: sensory information is perceived (seen, heard etc.)
- Stage 2: the sensory information is transferred to STM, where it is maintained by rehearsal (if it is not lost or replaced by new, incoming information)
- Stage 3: the information is transferred to LTM

Research evidence (Glanzer and Cunitz 1966)

Participants were asked to recall word lists. When words were recalled immediately, early and later words were more likely to be recalled (primacy and recency effect) due to STM and LTM effects. **Primacy effect** occurs because the first words are likely to have been transferred to LTM. **Recency effect** occurs because the last words in the list are still in STM. If there was a delay of 10 seconds or more before recall, there was only a primacy effect — only LTM was affected. This demonstrates a difference between STM and LTM.

Evaluation

Strengths
- The multi-store model is simple and can be tested. Research evidence supports the idea that STM and LTM are qualitatively different types of memory. Moreover, we have all, from time to time, 'rehearsed' information and it seems to make sense that rehearsed information is more likely to be remembered.

Limitations
- In real life, memories are created in contexts rather different from laboratory-based 'free recall' experiments, so perhaps this model does not explain fully the complexities of human memory. In addition, the model suggests that memory is a passive process, whereas theories of reconstructive memory suggest that memory is an active process.

Knowledge check 32

Write a definition of cognitive load.

The working memory model of memory

The Baddeley and Hitch (1974) model of working memory is more complex than the multi-store model, but it focuses solely on STM or, as Baddeley and Hitch call it, **working memory**. They propose a multi-store model of STM. In their model, STM is an active processor in which the central executive 'attends to and works on' either speech-based information passed to it from the articulatory–phonological loop or visually coded information passed to it by the visual system. The three components of this model are shown in Figure 2.

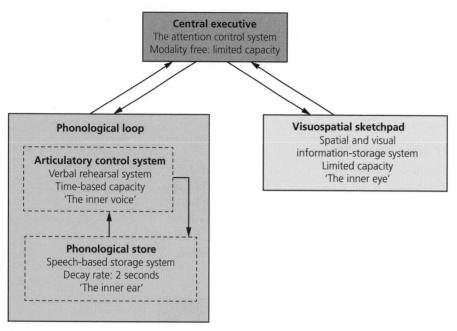

Figure 2 The working memory model

- The central executive processes information from all sensory routes — this process is 'attention-like', having limited capacity.
- The articulatory–phonological loop processes speech-based information. The phonological store focuses on speech perception (incoming speech) and the articulatory process focuses on speech production.
- The visuospatial **working area** (also known as the 'visuospatial sketchpad') is where spatial and visual information is processed.

The working memory model can be tested by the **interference task** technique. This technique is based on the assumption that the articulatory–phonological loop and the visuospatial scratchpad both have limited capacity to process information, so when participants are asked to perform two tasks, using the same system at the same time, their performance is affected.

> **Exam tip**
>
> Make sure you can suggest how the working memory model explains cognitive overload.

Evaluation

Strengths
- The working memory model suggests that rehearsal is an optional process, which is more realistic than the multi-store model, especially since we do not rehearse everything that we remember. The model can explain how we can successfully do two tasks at the same time if the tasks involve different stores, but why we have trouble performing two tasks at the same time if the tasks involve the same stores.

Limitations
- Least is known about the precise function of the most important component, the central executive, and the suggestion that there may be a single central executive may be inaccurate.

The impact of observation in the workplace

Much psychological research finds evidence that people change the way they behave when they are being watched. **Hint:** remember what you have learned about demand characteristics in experimental research.

The Hawthorne effect

The Hawthorne effect refers to the tendency of people to try harder and perform better when they are participants in an experiment. Individuals may change their behaviour due to the attention they are receiving from researchers rather than because of any manipulation of independent variables.

The effect was first described in the 1950s by researcher Henry A. Landsberger during his analysis of experiments conducted at the Hawthorne works electric company.

Social facilitation

Social facilitation happens when performance is altered due to the presence of other people and an audience can have a positive or negative effect on performance. Norman Triplett (1898) observed that cyclists performed better when they were racing against others cyclists than when racing only against the clock. In this study, Triplett claimed that the presence of other people competing in the same activity led to enhanced performance. However, in further research it was shown that some individuals performed tasks better even if they were only observed by an audience and therefore no effect of competition was needed. In addition, it was found that performance was increased only when participants thought the observers were evaluating them. This led researchers to believe that concern about how others are evaluating you is what causes social facilitation.

On the other hand, sometimes people perform worse on tasks when there are other people watching. In another study by Triplett (1898), children were given a task to operate a small piece of machinery, either in the presence of others or alone. Some children performed better alone, while others performed better with people watching. This showed that while some individuals were positively affected by the presence of others, some individuals were also negatively affected, yielding a decrease in performance. This negative effect on performance was explained by social psychologist Robert Zajonc.

Social facilitation theory

Zajonc (1965) proposed that being in the presence of others causes arousal, leading to an increase in performance. This idea is known as social facilitation theory. Zajonc (1965) states that given a task with other people present, the dominant (correct) response will be enhanced and the subordinate (incorrect) response will be inhibited. In a situation where the dominant response is mostly correct, such as if the task uses previously acquired skills, the subject will exhibit better performance. If the dominant response is mostly incorrect, such as learning a new task, then the subject will demonstrate poorer performance. Therefore, performance is improved with simple or familiar tasks, and deteriorates with complex or new tasks. This theory explains both the positive and negative effects of the presence of other people. In sum, social facilitation has been found to increase performance on simple, well-learned tasks and decrease performance of novel, difficult tasks.

Exam tip

Make sure you can explain why the Hawthorne effect is a disadvantage.

Knowledge check 33

What is meant by the 'Hawthorne effect'?

Exam tip

In an exam you might be given a hypothetical situation and asked to suggest whether having an audience will lead to better or worse performance.

Key research

Drews, F. A. and Doig, A. (2014) 'Evaluation of a configural vital sign display for intensive care unit nurses'

Method/Design: A configural vital sign (CVS) display developed based on studies of the cognitive work of ICU nurses. An independent measures design with the CVS display condition vs control traditional display.

Participants and sampling: 42 intensive care unit (ICU) nurses with a minimum 1 year's experience interpreted hypothetical patient data; 21 nurses were assigned to each condition: 69% of nurses were female with an age range of 25–64.

Design of CVS:

- Selection of variables to be included in the CVS display included systolic, diastolic and mean arterial blood pressure, heart rate and blood oxygen saturation. The goal of the CVS was to facilitate detection of abnormal trends in vital signs data.
- Based on interviews with nurses and data visualisation experts — the design requirements for the CVS included trend data, variability data reflecting changes in patient's vital signs, reduction of visual clutter and colour coding and geometric shapes to convey vital sign changes.
- Current state object (CSO) represented the current patient state by its shape and spatial location in a space of vital signs values. The size of the shapes and their relative position within the CSO demonstrate key information about the patient's current state and its extent of variability. Different colours were used to represent blood oxygen saturation.

Traditional display:

- A simplified version of an ICU display that consisted of the 'numerical data' section of the CVS display as a primary display. On request participants had access to trend information (not on the main screen like CVS).

Procedure:

- Four patient 'hypothetical' scenarios of early sepsis, septic shock, pulmonary embolus and a control stable scenario were developed to test speed and accuracy of accessing patient data using either of the display units. Scenarios were the same for all participants but their presentation order was randomised.
- Simulation took place at the University of Utah with a 20-minute training in the display unit. Participants were given 5 minutes to complete each scenario. Primary measures included the response time to come to an assessment and accuracy of data interpretation.

Results: Participants in the CVS display condition identified the patient's state more rapidly than in the control traditional display. There was a 30% improvement in response time to the CVS display. Nurses using the CVS display correctly identified the patient's condition more frequently than the control condition. Nurses rated the CVS display as having a lower mental demand than the traditional display.

Conclusions: Providing patient information in a CVS display that uses techniques of graphical display, colour coding and geometric shapes, improves speed and accuracy of data interpretation in the nurses who use it. The introduction of such displays into clinical monitoring has the potential to improve patient safety.

Reference: Drews, F. A. and Doig, A. (2014) 'Evaluation of a configural vital sign display for intensive care unit nurses', *Journal of Human Factors and Ergonomics Society*, 56 (3), 569–80

Application

You must be able to apply the research you have learned to suggest and explain at least one workplace design based on ergonomic research.

Reducing cognitive load

- Reduce the amount of load that is being placed on working memory by integrating the various sources of information, rather than giving information from several sources.
- Reduce the amount of unnecessary repetition load that is put on the working memory.
- Use visual and auditory techniques to increase short-term memory capacity.
- Remove unnecessary visual elements because these increase the cognitive load as they need to be processed.
- Use chunking by breaking the information or task down into chunks to reduce the number of things that have to be attended to at once.
- Reduce the number of choices needed to make a decision because the time it takes to make a decision increases with the number of choices available.

Observation in the workplace

Contemporary research suggests that it does not take a human being to make us feel as if we are being watched. All it takes is an image of a pair of human eyes.

Research evidence: Ernest-Jones et al. (2011)

Laboratory studies have shown that images of eyes can cause people to behave more cooperatively. This research looked at the effect of eye images on cooperative behaviour in a novel context — littering behaviour in a university cafeteria. The study attempted to discover the mechanism by which they work, by displaying eye images associated with, and not associated with, verbal messages to clear litter. The research found a 50% reduction in littering in the presence of posters featuring eyes, as compared to posters featuring flowers. This effect was independent of whether the poster asked for litter clearing or contained an unrelated message, suggesting that the effect of eye images is not to draw attention to verbal instructions. There was some support for the hypothesis that eye images had a larger effect when there were fewer people in the café than when the café was busy. The results confirm that the effects of subtle cues of observation on cooperative behaviour can be significant.

> **Knowledge check 34**
>
> When designing a visual display, what changes can be made to a display of information to make it easier to read?

Psychological effects of built environment (Social)

This topic looks at the impact of the built environment and urban renewal on our wellbeing. The key research is by Ulrich (1984) who looked at how a view through a window may influence recovery from surgery.

Research into health and wellbeing in the built environment addresses the positive and negative effects from people-environment interactions. Understanding the role of the environment, particularly the built environment, and its effect on human health and wellbeing, can help to improve people's quality of life.

Exam tip

You must be able to suggest and explain at least one example of environmental design used to improve health/wellbeing.

The built environment

The physical aspect of an urban environment is presumed to affect residents' behaviour. Cities can be very stressful because noise, traffic density and pollution usually are greater than in rural places. However, cities have cultural and social benefits and a greater choice of employment. Environmental psychology shows that the physical qualities of the urban environment are important.

Pruitt–Igoe

Pruitt–Igoe was a vast urban housing project built in the 1950s in the US city of St. Louis, Missouri. The scale of the project was huge: 33 buildings, 11-storeys each, arranged across 57 acres. The complex was supposed to put the modernist ideals of Le Corbusier into action replacing the city slums with 'vertical neighbourhoods for poor people'. Living conditions in Pruitt–Igoe began to decline soon after its completion in 1956. By the late 1960s, the complex had become internationally infamous for its poverty, crime and segregation and in the 1970s the buildings were demolished with explosives. Pruitt–Igoe became an icon of urban renewal and public-policy planning failure. Charles Jencks, an architectural theorist, suggested that the demolition of Pruitt–Igoe was 'the day that Modern Architecture died'.

Consequences of living in high-rise buildings

Gifford (2007) summarised the results of research on the influences of high-rise buildings on residents' experiences of the building, satisfaction, preferences, social behaviour, crime and fear of crime, children, mental health and suicide. Although there are moderating factors, including socioeconomic status, parenting, gender and the ability to choose a housing form, the literature suggests that high rises are less satisfactory than other housing forms for most people. They are not optimal for children, social relations are more impersonal and helping behaviour is less than in other housing forms. Crime and fear of crime are greater in them and they may independently account for some suicides.

Knowledge check 35

According to Gifford (2007) what are the consequences of high-rise living?

Contemporary urban renewal

Rachel and Steven Kaplan (1980s) researched the effect of nature on people's relationships and health. Their work on 'restorative environments' and attention restoration theory (ART) had an impact on how landscape and design professionals and others view humanity's relationship with nature. ART asserts that people can concentrate better after spending time in nature, or even looking at scenes of nature. The Kaplans' research has found that office workers with a view of nature are happier and healthier at work (Kaplan 1993). Exposure to natural environments has proven to lift people's moods and enhance their ability to concentrate. Also, there is evidence to suggest that public open space should be designed in terms of networks of small linked spaces of various kinds, and that this kind of spatial arrangement may have a restorative potential arising from its capacity to facilitate social interaction.

Healthcare environments

The design of these environments can hinder people's recovery, through noises disturbing sleep, poor lighting, and materials and systems harbouring bacteria. Wood (2013) found staff satisfaction with the built environment in inpatient psychiatric wards was highest in wards with modern features such as a no-corridor design and personal bathrooms. The ability to observe patients, exterior views and good staff facilities were not associated with staff satisfaction.

Key research

Ulrich (1984) 'Views through a window influence recovery from surgery'

Method and Design: A field study where patients are matched into two groups of a view of either a 'natural scene' or 'brick wall'. Matching was on sex, age, smoking status, weight, year of surgery and floor level. A 'blind' design was used where the recovery data were extracted by a nurse who was unaware of the different view of patient's records.

Participants: Records of recovery were taken from patients who had undergone gall bladder surgery at a Pennsylvania hospital. Patients were between 20 and 69 years and had no history of psychological disturbances. The final database consisted of records of 46 patients grouped into 23 pairs (15 female and 8 male).

Procedure: Data were collected between 1 May and 20 October ,1972–81. Records were of patients assigned to rooms on the second and third floors where windows either looked out on a small stand of deciduous trees or a brown brick wall. The same nurses were assigned to all rooms on each floor. All rooms were identical other than the view in terms of arrangement and physical characteristics. The only thing that differed was the view seen through the window, visible while in bed. Five types of information were taken from each record: length of hospitalisation (days), number and strength of analgesics required each day, number and strength of anxiety medication per day, minor complications and all nurses' notes relating to each patient's condition.

Results: Patients with the window views of the trees spent less time in the hospital than those with views of the brick wall (7.96 vs 8.7 days). Nurses' comments were categorised into positive (e.g in good spirits) or negative (e.g. upset). More negative comments were made on patients with the brick wall (3.96 compared to 1.13 with the tree view). On days 2 to 5, tree view patients took fewer pain doses than those in the wall view group but there was no significant difference in anxiety medication.

→

Conclusions: Patients with the tree view had shorter post-operative stays, fewer negative comments and took fewer strong pain doses of medication. The natural scene through the window thus had some therapeutic influence. It must be noted that the 'built' view in this study was monotonous and thus the conclusion cannot extend to all urban views that may present a lively city view.

Reference: Ulrich, R. S. (1984) 'View through a window may influence recovery from surgery', *Science, New Series*, 224 (4647), 420–21

Knowledge check 36

Suggest one advantage of the research method used by Ulrich (1984).

Application

You must be able to suggest ways by which the built environment influences wellbeing and suggest and explain at least one example of environmental design used to improve health/wellbeing.

Exam tip

You could be asked to redesign an urban space. Make sure you can give one suggestion as to what to include in the design in order to foster community wellbeing.

Territory and personal space (Social)

This topic focuses on territory and personal space in the workplace. The key research is Wells (2000) 'Office clutter or meaningful personal displays: the role of office personalisation in employee and organisational wellbeing'.

Personal space

Personal space can be defined as an area with invisible boundaries into which strangers may not come. Personal space can be seen as an invisible bubble that surrounds us and that expands or contracts depending on our social situation.

Hall (1914–2009) developed the concept of 'Proxemics'. He divided the personal distance we keep from others into four main zones. These zones serve as reaction zones and when you enter a specific zone, you automatically activate certain psychological and physical reactions in that person.

- **Public distance zone:** this outer bubble is usually larger than 3.6 metres. It is reserved for public speaking, or when talking to a large group.
- **Social distance zone:** this space is between 1.5 and 3 metres. It is the most neutral and comfortable zone to start a conversation between people who do not know each other well. It is the distance you keep from strangers that you may have some interaction with shopkeepers or service providers.
- **Personal distance zone:** this zone ranges from 60 cm to 1.5 metres. This space is reserved for friends and family — people you know and trust.
- **Intimate distance zone:** this ranges from direct contact to 60 cm. This space is reserved for the most trusted and loved in our social circles, partners and siblings. This space is like a private bubble and if a stranger is that close we may feel anxious and even enter flight-or-fight mode.

Factors that influence personal space

How we use personal space and how frequently our personal space is 'invaded' will be a function of the design of the physical environment. For example, cramped seating spaces, the number of people sharing a small office, and shop layout will all determine

Exam tip

You must be able to suggest and explain at least one office design strategy based on research into territory or personal space.

the level of interpersonal space invasion that occurs. However, there are individual differences in personal space:

- **Gender:** males interacting with other males require the largest interpersonal distance, followed by females interacting with other females, and finally males interacting with females (Gifford 1987).
- **Age:** personal space gets bigger as we grow older (Hayduk 1983). Children tend to be quite happy to be physically close to each other, but this changes as awareness of adult sexuality develops.
- **Culture:** Hall (1959) identified the importance of cultural variation. He suggested that while all cultures use personal space to communicate, and tend to conform to the different categories, the size of the space within the categories varies across cultures.
- **Personality:** there is some evidence of personality difference. Extraverted persons tend to require smaller personal space, while introverted people require a larger interpersonal distance (Gifford 1982).
- **Situational effects on personal space:** where the general tone of the interaction is friendly, we are more willing to decrease our personal space requirement but where the tone of the interaction is unfriendly, people move further apart.
- **Competition and cooperation:** the cooperation versus competition effects on personal space interact with orientation. Generally, people in cooperation will select a smaller interpersonal distance unless the competition requires interpersonal contact.
- **Status:** the greater the difference in status between individuals, the larger the interpersonal distance used.
- **Expectations and social perception:** the type of person we are going to meet in a situation influences our choice of interpersonal distance. When we anticipate meeting a warm and friendly person we choose smaller distances.

Knowledge check 37

Suggest the type of social interactions that might take place in the social distance zone.

Territory

Sommer (1969) makes the distinction between personal space and territory: the most important difference is that personal space is carried around with us while territory is relatively stationary. The animal or man will usually mark the boundaries of his territory so that they are visible to others, but the boundaries of personal space are invisible. Personal space has the body as its centre, while territory does not. Animals will usually fight to maintain dominion over their territory but will withdraw if others intrude into their personal space. Except in war people do not usually fight over territory.

Seating arrangements

Socio-architecture is a phrase coined by psychologist Osmond (1957) who also coined the terms sociopetal and sociofugal to describe seating arrangement that encouraged or discouraged social interaction. **Sociofugal** and **sociopetal** describe two types of seating arrangement: sociofugal arrangements promote seclusion and discourage social interaction by having the seating facing outwards, and sociopetal arrangements encourage social interaction by having the seating facing into a group.

Exam tip

When describing a seating arrangement, in terms of social interaction, make sure you can describe the difference between a sociopetal and a sociofugal seating arrangement.

Workplace territoriality

Organisations spend millions designing workspaces and managing conflict, negative emotions and behaviour caused by workplace territoriality. This issue can be especially acute in open-plan offices, and in offices where employees are expected to 'share space'. Employees may use strategies to mark their territory, by using personal possessions as territory markers. For example, teachers often define areas in the staff room as their 'personal territory' and new staff members soon learn that 'that seat is George's'.

Open-plan offices

Open-plan offices are favoured by companies because more employees can be housed in a smaller space and there are also supposed communication benefits. **Kim et al. (2013)** asked employees to rate their satisfaction with seven aspects of their office environment including: temperature, lighting, privacy and ease of interaction, and their overall satisfaction with their personal workspace. Two thirds of the surveyed workers were based in open-plan offices (with or without partial partitions); a quarter had private offices; and a few shared a single room with co-workers. Overall, workers in private offices were the most satisfied with their workspace and workers in open-plan offices expressed strong dissatisfaction with sound privacy. The most powerful factor associated with overall satisfaction levels was 'amount of space'. Noise was strongly associated with satisfaction for open-plan office workers whereas light and ease of interaction were more strongly associated with satisfaction for workers in private offices.

Exam tip

Make sure you can suggest factors that increase or decrease satisfaction with open-plan offices and/or workplaces.

Open-plan offices can be bad for health

A survey by Canada Life suggests that open-plan offices may be detrimental to an employee's health, wellbeing and productivity. Only 6.1% surveyed thought it was healthy to be in an open-plan environment and just 6.5% thought it was productive. In the survey, those employees who worked in open-plan offices took over 70% more sick days than those who worked from home. Also research shows that 85% of people who work in open-plan offices are dissatisfied with their working environment and cannot concentrate. Of those surveyed, 95% said working privately was important, but only 41% said they could do so, and 31% had to leave the office to get work completed. More than 10,000 workers across 14 countries were surveyed, and findings showed that open-plan office workers lose 86 minutes a day due to distractions, many employees are unmotivated, unproductive and stressed and have little capacity to think and work creatively.

Knowledge check 38

Outline what employees may dislike about open-plan office space.

Key research

Wells (2000) 'Office clutter or meaningful personal displays: the role of office personalisation in employee and organisational wellbeing'

Method/Design: A survey based study with 5 out of 20 companies also participating as case studies where employees were interviewed about the importance of personal items and the effects on wellbeing. An observation checklist was used to check the number of personal items.

Participants/Sampling: A group of office workers at 20 companies in Orange County, California, were recruited from 2,000 companies participating in a small business project. The 20 companies included two manufacturing companies, two real estate agencies, a law firm and a car dealership. The 338 respondents consisted of 187 males, 138 females and 13 gender unspecified who were aged between 25 and 44 years.

Procedure: employee survey:

- **Section 1** examined workspace personalisation and consisted of the number of personal items displayed, the types of items displayed, the degree they would like to display items but are not allowed, the extent of workspace arrangement, the reasons for personalising workspace or not and the extent of personalisation of team spaces.
- **Section 2** assessed satisfaction with physical work environment (using 5-point rating scales).
- **Section 3** assessed job satisfaction (5-point rating scale).
- **Section 4** assessed physical and psychological wellbeing using general wellbeing questions such as 'how do you feel about your life as a whole?'
- **Section 5** assessed employee perceptions of organisational wellbeing, including social climate, moral and productivity.
- **Section 6** assessed personality traits and the need for affiliation, privacy and creativity.

Results: Men and women personalise for different reasons with women using it to express identities and emotions and men to show their status. The data supported the view that personalisation was more important to women for general wellbeing. Most people display symbols of personal relationships (68%) with the lowest being music (3%). Personalisation is significantly associated with satisfaction of work environment but this was not found with personalisation of team spaces. Satisfaction with physical work environment was also positively associated with job satisfaction. Companies that allow more personalisation have a more positive organisational climate.

Conclusions: The difference in importance of personalisation to men and women may be due to the needs related to it, for example women who have traditionally been homemakers feel more of a need to make their environments at work comfortable. Women may also feel more of a need to express their identities as the workplace has a male aura. Business managers may benefit from this study by realising that people want to personalise their workspaces and restricting this may be linked to reduced satisfaction of the work environment and job.

Summary: Even when organisations have clear policies restricting personalisation of office space, employees do it anyway. There seems to a strong, psychological need for people to personalise their workspaces. Not only is personalisation beneficial for employees, it is also beneficial for organisations. Companies that allow employees to personalise their work space have higher levels of employee morale, better social climates and reduced turnover.

Reference: Wells, M. M. (2000) 'Office clutter or meaningful personal displays: the role of office personalisation in employee and organisational wellbeing', *Journal of Environmental Psychology*, 20 (3), 239–55

Content Guidance

Application

You must be able to suggest and explain at least one office design strategy based on research into territory or personal space.

Exam tip

Make sure you can suggest why men and women personalise their office spaces.

Summary

You should be able to:
- describe concepts, theories and studies specified by the indicative content:
  - stressors in the environment
  - biological rhythms
  - recycling and other conservation behaviours
  - ergonomics: human factors
  - psychological effects of the built environment
  - territory and personal space
- apply the methodological issues and debates in psychology
- recognise the contribution the key research has made to the topic
- apply the background, research and application to novel situations
- consider how different areas of psychology can inform our understanding of applied psychology
- explore social, moral, cultural and spiritual issues where applicable
- recognise how the research contributes to an understanding of individual, social and cultural diversity
- recognise how society makes decisions about scientific issues how psychology is useful in society

When answering questions on applied psychology you will be expected to illustrate your answers with knowledge and understanding of the issues and debates in psychology.

Questions & Answers

This section is not intended as a set of model answers to possible examination questions, or as an account of the right material to include in any examination question. It is intended simply to give you an idea of how your examination is structured and how you might improve your examination performance. You should read through the relevant topic in the Content Guidance before you attempt a question from the Question and Answers section. Look at the sample answers only after you have tackled the question yourself.

You will take the Applied Psychology Paper 3 exam at the end of your 2-year A-level course. The exam includes synoptic questions to allow you to demonstrate your ability to draw together your skill, knowledge and understanding from across the full course and to provide extended responses.

Paper 3 Applied Psychology

Paper 3 is assessed in a written 2-hour exam in which 105 marks are awarded, comprising 35% of the A-level. There are two sections in the exam:

- **Section A** comprises questions on issues in mental health — 35 marks are awarded and you must answer all questions.
- **Section B** comprises questions on the applied options: child psychology, criminal psychology, environmental psychology and sport and exercise psychology. You must answer questions on **TWO** applied options. Each applied option has synoptic questions worth 35 marks.

This book only includes the Section B topics of criminal psychology and environmental psychology.

Assessment objectives: AO1, AO2 and AO3 skills

Assessment objectives (AOs) are set by Ofqual and are the same across all A-level psychology specifications and all exam boards. The exams measure how students have achieved the following assessment objectives:

- **AO1:** Demonstrate knowledge and understanding of scientific ideas, processes, techniques and procedures.
- **AO2:** Apply knowledge and understanding of scientific ideas, processes, techniques and procedures in a theoretical context; in a practical context; when handling qualitative data and quantitative data.
- **AO3:** Analyse, interpret and evaluate scientific information, ideas and evidence, including in relation to issues, to make judgements and reach conclusions and to develop and refine practical design and procedures.

AO1 questions
Identify or **outline** or **describe**…

A03 questions

Compare a physiological explanation with any one other explanation of mental illness.

A01 + A03 questions

Discuss the nature/nurture debate in relation to causes of criminal behaviour.

A01 + A02 + A03 questions

Assess the methodological issues involved in researching the impact of the built environment.

Effective examination performance

Read the question carefully because marks are awarded only for the specific requirements of the question *as it is set*. Do not waste valuable time answering a question that you *wish* had been set.

For extended answer questions, make a brief plan before you start writing. There is space on the exam paper for planning and a plan can be as simple as a list of points, but you must know what, and how much, you plan to write. Time management in exams is vital.

Sometimes a question asks you to outline something. You should practise doing this in order to develop the skill of précis. Be aware of the difference between AO1, AO2 and AO3 commands (injunctions). You will lose marks if you treat AO3 commands such as 'discuss' as an opportunity to write more descriptive (AO1) content. Read the question command carefully and note the relevant skill requirement in your question plan.

Marks are awarded in **bands** for:

- **AO1:** the amount of relevant material presented, where low marks are awarded for brief or inappropriate material and high marks for accurate and detailed material.
- **AO2:** the level and effectiveness of critical commentary, where low marks are awarded for superficial consideration of a restricted range of issues and high marks for a good range of ideas and specialist terms, and effective use of material addressing a broad range of issues.
- **AO3:** the extent to which the answer demonstrates a thorough understanding of methods by which psychologists conduct research, for analysis, interpretation, explanation and evaluation of research methodologies and investigative activities.

Questions in this guide

Questions are presented in examination style, and this section is structured as follows:

- example questions for Section A: issues in mental health and Section B: options in the style of the Paper 3 exam
- example student responses at grade A/B (Student A), demonstrating thorough knowledge, good understanding and an ability to deal with the data presented in the question
- example student responses at grade C/D (Student B), demonstrating strengths and weaknesses and the potential for improvement

Where a question is marked with * this indicates that the question requires a synoptic response and you may include in your answer material that you have learned across the whole 2-year course.

Exam comments

All student responses are followed by comments. These are preceded by the icon **e**. These comments may indicate where credit is due, strengths in the answer, areas for improvement, specific problems, common errors, lack of clarity, irrelevance, mistakes in meanings of terms and/or misinterpretation of the question. Comments may also indicate how example answers might be marked in an exam. Exam comments on the questions are preceded by the icon **e**. They offer tips on what you need to do to gain full marks.

Section A: issues in mental health

In the exam you must answer all the questions in Section A. * indicates that the question requires a synoptic response.

Note: the questions are numbered as they would be on the Component 3 exam paper.

1 a Outline the characteristics of any **one** disorder. (2 marks)

(e) The question injunction is 'outline' so it assesses AO1 skills. To access full marks the answer must include the characteristics that have been cited in psychological literature. Your answer could include: the characteristics of an affective (mood) disorder, an anxiety disorder or a psychotic disorder.

Student A

Clinical depression is a mood or 'affective' disorder in which a negative emotional state influences perceptions, thoughts and behaviour. Diagnosis requires symptoms such as extreme sadness, tearfulness, depressed mood and loss of interest in usual activities. As well as these symptoms, depression may involve disturbed sleep and appetite, lack of energy as well as negative self-concept, feelings of guilt, low self-esteem and anxiety.

(e) **2/2 marks awarded.** This is a clear, detailed and accurate description of the characteristics of an affective disorder (depression).

Student B

Clinical depression is a disorder involving sadness, tearfulness, depressed mood and loss of interest in usual activities as well as loss of appetite.

(e) **1/2 marks awarded.** This answer is brief and anecdotal and could have been written by someone who had not studied psychology.

b Explain how situational factors can influence the diagnoses of mental disorders. (3 marks)

(e) The question injunction is 'explain' but the question assesses AO1 skills. To access full marks you must explain how cultural bias can influence the diagnosis of mental disorders.

Student A

One definition of abnormality is as behaviour which deviates from the social norm and because the behaviour of some people does not fit in with social norms they are seen as different or 'ill'. [a] However, behaviour is judged as normal or abnormal depending on the situation in which it is observed. For example, Rosenhan found that normal behaviour, like waiting early for lunch, was seen as abnormal inside a psychiatric hospital. [b] Thus the social situation in which a patient is observed may influence the diagnosis. [c]

[e] **3/3 marks awarded.** This is a clear, detailed and accurate explanation of how situational factors may influence diagnosis. In [a] the student gives an accurate outline of the definition of abnormality. In [b] and [c] the answer gives a clear explanation of how the situation of the patient may influence diagnosis.

Student B

Rosenhan found that normal behaviour, like waiting early for lunch, was seen as abnormal inside a psychiatric hospital. [a] Thus if the patient is seen inside a psychiatric hospital their behaviour may be judged as abnormal. The social situation in which a patient is observed may influence the diagnosis. [b]

[e] **1–2/3 marks awarded.** This is a rather circular explanation that could be written more clearly.

2 **According to Szasz (2011) 'the term "mental illness" refers to the subjective judgements of some persons about the behaviours of other persons'.**

With reference to the key research, discuss whether alternatives to the medical model of mental illness support the idea that psychology is a science. (5 marks)

[e] The question injunction is 'discuss' so it assesses AO1 and AO3 skills.

There is 1 AO1 mark for demonstrating knowledge and understanding through reference to the Szasz study.

There are 4 AO3 marks for analysis of what is meant by 'psychology as a science' and discussion of how at least two alternatives to the medical model of mental illness contribute (or not) to the debate about psychology as a science. **The discussion must focus on more than one alternate explanation to the medical model.**

Your answer must be explanatory rather than descriptive and could include:

- a brief explanation of science and scientific methods
- an evaluation of the behaviourist explanation as scientific or not
- an evaluation of the cognitive explanation as scientific or not
- an evaluation of the psychodynamic or humanist explanation as scientific or not
- a discussion as to the value of 'being scientific'

Student A

The scientific method involves testing hypotheses and collecting data in controlled experimental conditions. The scientific method is objective and unbiased and should be able to demonstrate cause-and-effect relationships in which the subjective opinions of the researcher had no influence. a Arguably, the medical model is the most scientific explanation for mental illness as this model relies on experimental methods and studies objective biological facts such as genes and biochemistry to explain mental illness. b In his paper Szasz suggests that: 'If all the conditions now called mental illnesses have biological causes, the term mental illness is meaningless.' What Szasz seems to be saying is that if the biological model could explain all mental illness there would be no need for psychology, as a study of the 'mind'. c

Perhaps the least scientific explanation of mental illness is the psychodynamic approach in which Freud suggests unconscious motivation for behaviour and that unacceptable desires originating in the id are repressed by defence mechanisms to reduce anxiety. Psychodynamic research usually gathers qualitative self-report data that may be subject to biased interpretation. Such evidence, usually based on case studies, is not based on falsifiable hypotheses, and thus does not support the idea that psychology is a science. d Equally, cognitive explanations, based on the idea that mental illness is caused by faulty or irrational thought processes, and in which the focus is on understanding how the individual subjectively experiences the world, cannot be said to be scientific. Minds are hypothetical constructs and as such it is difficult to gain an objective measurement of mental processes. Also, most cognitive research relies on asking people to self-report their feelings and beliefs and people may not always, even if they know it, tell the truth about their thought processes. e However, because the medical model cannot show that all mental illnesses are caused by genes, or brain diseases, even if alternative explanations do not support the idea that psychology is a science these explanations are useful. f Also, when scientific research isolates one variable (the independent variable) to study the effect on another variable (dependent variable) it is always reductionist and the study of human behaviour, especially mental illness, requires an understanding of the complex ways that biological, environmental, social and cognitive factors interact. This understanding may be best served by including unscientific theories and methods in the research process. g As Szasz says, 'people said to have mental illness may be benefited by persons who respect them and help them' and this is true even if unscientific methods such as 'talking cures' are used. h

e **5/5 marks awarded.** Student A has written a thorough and in-depth discussion. In a the student gives an accurate outline of what is meant by science. In b the student suggests a reason why the medical model is the most scientific explanation of mental illness. In c the student links the Szasz paper to the idea that the medical model could invalidate psychology. In d and e the student explains why both the psychodynamic and cognitive explanations of mental illness are not scientific. In f, g and h the student gives a knowledgeable argument that although unscientific, alternative explanations for mental illness are necessary and useful. But, the answer is too long for a 5-mark question and would probably have been awarded 4 or 5 marks had it stopped at j.

Student B

The scientific method is objective and should be able to demonstrate cause-and-effect relationships in which the subjective opinions of the researcher have no influence. a Perhaps the least scientific explanation of mental illness is the psychodynamic approach which usually gathers qualitative self-report data that may be subject to biased interpretation. Such evidence cannot support the idea that psychology is a science. b Also, cognitive explanations, based on the idea that mental illness is caused by faulty or irrational thought processes cannot be said to be scientific. Minds are hypothetical constructs and it is difficult to gain a valid and objective measurement of mental processes. Most cognitive research relies on asking people to self-report their feelings and beliefs and people may not always tell the truth. c However, at present, the medical model cannot show that all mental illness has a biological cause so even if alternative explanations do not support the idea that psychology is a science these explanations are useful. d

---

e **3/5 marks awarded.** Student B has not referred to the key study by Szasz. The answer is an accurate but brief discussion. In a, b and c Student B has given a basic outline demonstrating why both the psychodynamic and cognitive explanations of mental illness are not scientific. In d the student suggests that even if alternative explanations for mental illness are unscientific these are useful.

3   Explain how behaviourist treatment is used to treat one specific disorder.   (5 marks)

e The question injunction is 'explain'. This question assesses AO2 skills, so marks are awarded if you apply your knowledge and understanding to an unfamiliar situation. Answers are likely to suggest systematic desensitisation or token economy. Detailed knowledge will include a description of the treatment process and an explanation of why it is effective.

Your answer could include:

- a brief explanation of the assumptions of the behaviourist approach
- a description of the process of systematic desensitisation (or token economy)
- an identification of elements in the hierarchy of fears
- how clients learn to associate pleasant relaxation with fear-provoking situations
- the step-by-step approach through the hierarchy of fears

Your answer must be explanatory rather than descriptive and you are not expected to provide more than 5 minutes of writing.

Student A

Based on the assumption that mental disorders are learned and can be unlearned, behaviourist treatments are effective with anxiety disorders such as phobias. **a** Treatment based on operant conditioning assumes that behaviour that brings about pleasurable consequences is likely to be repeated and usually involves the positive reinforcement of 'normal' behaviour. **b** An example of a behaviourist treatment is systematic desensitisation, in which phobics can gradually be reintroduced to a feared object or situation. **c** Systematic desensitisation is behaviourist therapy where the disorder, for instance a person's phobia, is broken down into the stimulus–response units that comprise it. In treating a phobia by systematic desensitisation, the patient constructs a hierarchy of fears and is then trained to relax while in the presence of the phobic object (e.g. spider). **d** For instance, in a phobia of spiders, the least stressful situation might be to look at a picture of a spider and the most stressful might be to have to touch a spider. **e** The therapist works though each unit in the ascending hierarchy, helping the person to replace each phobic response of fear, with the response of feeling relaxed. **f** In effect, step by step, the phobia is unlearned as, instead of fear in the presence of the phobic object, the patient learns to feel pleasure and relaxation. **g** McGrath et al. (1990) reported that following systematic desensitisation 70% of phobic patients show improvement in symptoms. **h**

e **5/5 marks awarded.** This answer shows good application. A clear, detailed and accurate behaviourist treatment is a specified for a named disorder. Student A has given an effective and accurate explanation of the assumptions of and process of systematic desensitisation and has applied this to the treatment of an anxiety disorder (phobia). The strength of this answer is that in **a** to **c** the student accurately outlines the behaviourist assumptions and identifies the treatment as systematic desensitisation. In **d** to **f** the process involved in systematic desensitisation is explained and in **g** the student explains why systematic desensitisation is effective. **h** added little to the answer and was not necessary.

Student B

One behaviourist treatment is systematic desensitisation which can be used to treat phobias **a**. Systematic desensitisation helps people to gradually learn to associate a feared stimulus such as a snake with a pleasant response such as relaxation. **b** The person with the phobia works with a therapist to learn to relax and eventually the fear will be cured.

e **2/5 marks awarded.** In this answer there is limited application of a behaviourist treatment with little reference to the treatment of any disorder. Student B has given a basic outline demonstrating some relevant knowledge and understanding, but the answer is descriptive rather than explanatory and should be more detailed and much more clearly applied to explain how and why systematic desensitisation is effective.

4* Compare the biological explanation with **one** other explanation of mental illness. (10 marks)

ⓔ The question injunction is 'compare'. This question assesses AO1 and AO3 skills.

AO1 (5 marks): Demonstration of knowledge and understanding of the biological explanation is likely to be achieved through suggesting that genes, biochemical processes and/or brain structures are the reason for a mental illness. Answers could consider one explanation or more than one and may explain how biological processes cause disorders such as schizophrenia or depression. The answer may outline a specific disorder and or may use empirical evidence as elaboration of the comparison.

AO3 (5 marks): Ideas and evidence relating to the biological explanation must be compared with at least one other explanation, for example the behaviourist or cognitive explanation. The answer may compare the explanations using any issue or debate, such as the explanation adopting a reductionist or holistic view or using the nature vs nurture debate, or on methodological issues such as the type of research supporting the explanation. Each point should be clearly identified, and linked to both explanations. Empirical evidence is only creditworthy where it is appropriately used to support the similarity or difference being discussed.

Student A

Biological explanations suggest that mental illness is caused by biochemistry, genetics and/or brain anatomy. For example, that an excess of the neurotransmitter dopamine is thought to be involved in schizophrenia. Also, serotonin is the chemical in the brain thought to be involved in regulating anxiety, and medications known as Selective Serotonin Re-uptake Inhibitors (SSRIs) are often used to treat anxiety disorders. Some mental disorders, such as schizophrenia, run in families, suggesting an underlying genetic abnormality and Kety found that the incidence of schizophrenia was ten times higher in the biological relatives of the schizophrenic adoptees than in the biological relatives of a control group. ⓐ

In contrast to biological explanations, behaviourist explanations make three assumptions. First, that all behaviour is learned, second, that what has been learned can be unlearned, and third that abnormal behaviour is learned in the same way as normal behaviour. **Unlike the biological explanation**, this model sees abnormal behaviour as the problem and not as a symptom of some underlying biological cause. ⓑ **In contrast to biochemical explanations**, behaviourists propose that classical conditioning can explain anxiety disorders such as phobias, and in the case of Little Albert, Watson and Rayner (1920) demonstrated how classical conditioning could explain the way in which fear could be learned. ⓒ Biological explanations take a nature not nurture approach to mental illness, suggesting that some people are 'born' to become mentally ill and there is little or nothing they can do about it. **In contrast to the biological approach**, behaviourist explanations take a nurture not nature approach to mental illness, suggesting that the abnormal behaviour in mental illness can be unlearned. [d] **For different reasons** both biological explanations and behaviourist explanations of mental illness are **reductionist**. Biological explanations focus on biological facts and ignore the complex relationships between biology and the cognitive and social factors involved in mental illness. **Similarly**, behaviourist approaches suggesting stimulus-response learning involve environmental reductionism because behaviourists reduce mental illness to observable behaviour, ignoring biological and cognitive influences on behaviour. [e] **However**, the scientific status of the medical profession means that biological explanations are credible and objective evidence shows that biological causes can be linked to the symptoms of mental illness. **Whereas**, although the behaviourist approach is hopeful as it predicts that people with mental illness can change (relearn) their behaviour, and behaviourist treatment, such as systematic desensitisation, is effective with phobic patients, behaviourists cannot explain all psychological disorders. [f]

e **9/10 marks awarded.** Student A gives a strong answer and in [a] and [b] shows a good understanding of the key assumptions of both a biological and the behaviourist explanation of mental illness. In [c], [d], [e] and [f] points of comparison (similarities and/or differences) are clearly identified and referenced appropriately to both biological and behaviourist explanations. There is a well-developed line of reasoning which is clear and logically structured. The information presented is relevant and argued effectively.

Student B

Biological explanations suggest that mental illness is caused by biochemistry, genetics and/or brain anatomy. For example, an excess of the neurotransmitter dopamine is thought to be involved in schizophrenia. Also, some mental disorders, such as schizophrenia, run in families, suggesting an underlying genetic abnormality. [a] In contrast to biological explanations, behaviourist explanations suggest that mental illness is learned. [b] For example, behaviourists propose that classical conditioning can explain anxiety disorders such as phobias. [c] **Unlike** behaviourist explanations, biological explanations take a nature not nurture approach to mental illness, suggesting that some people are 'born' to become mentally ill and there is little or nothing they can do about it. [d] **Both** biological explanations and behaviourist explanations of mental illness are **reductionist**. Biological explanations focus only on biological facts and behaviourist explanations reduce mental illness to stimulus-response learning, ignoring biological and cognitive influences on behaviour. [e]

e **5/10 marks awarded.** In [a] to [c] the student gives a brief and limited description of the key assumptions of both the biological and behaviourist explanation of mental illness. The answer lacks detail and, especially the behaviourist explanation, is superficial. Points of comparison are made, but in [d] and [e] the comparisons could have been expanded, explained and argued more effectively. The information is relevant but lacks explanation.

5* Discuss the reductionism/holism debate in relation to the biological explanation of mental illness. (10 marks)

e The question injunction is 'discuss'. This question assesses AO2 and AO3 skills.

AO2 (5 marks): In order to demonstrate application of knowledge and understanding in a theoretical context, your answer could outline the two sides of the reductionism/holism debate and relate it to how the biological explanation is usually considered reductionist, probably with an application of biological explanations for mental illness. Less detailed explanations that just identify the reductionist/holism debate with a link to biological assumptions of mental illness are likely to gain mid-band marks.

AO3 (5 marks): You can show analytical and evaluative skills by considering the effect of the biological approach being considered as reductionist in terms of lack of responsibility, and ethical/deterministic issues such as gene testing can be considered. Another way the reductionism/holism debate could be discussed might be to consider the advantages of reductionist/biological explanations as being scientific and leading to advances in scientific treatments for mental illness.

For 9–10 marks, a good explanation of the reductionism/holism debate is explicitly applied to the biological explanation of mental illness. There is a detailed discussion of the debate in relation to the biological explanation of mental illness with a well-developed line of reasoning which is clear, logically structured and the information presented is relevant and substantiated by evidence.

Plan your answer, and write about four paragraphs. Each paragraph should explain and argue a point linking the reductionism/holism debate to the biological explanation of mental illness.

■ Section B: options

Note: the questions are numbered as they would be on the Component 3 exam paper.

Option 2: criminal psychology

In Section B every question requires a synoptic response and you must answer all parts of the question.

7   a*   Explain how the 'broken windows' research by Wilson and Kelling (1982) could be used to reduce crime.   (10 marks)

ⓔ The question injunction is 'explain'. This question assesses AO1 and AO2 skills.

AO1 (5 marks): You must demonstrate knowledge and understanding of scientific ideas, processes, techniques and procedures. To access the top band you must refer to the broken windows study by Wilson and Kelling. To demonstrate knowledge and understanding of the key study you must describe the research clearly and effectively.

AO2 (5 marks): You must apply your knowledge and understanding of scientific ideas, processes, techniques and procedures. You should apply your knowledge and understanding of the broken windows theory by suggesting how the research can be applied to reduce crime. Your answer should focus on the application of the broken windows theory, and could show how changing the features of a neighbourhood can increase or decrease crime and how a zero tolerance policy can reduce crime.

Student A

Wilson and Kelling suggest that crime will increase in neighbourhoods where vandalism occurs. They suggest that if signs of decay, such as broken windows, are not repaired vandals are likely to break more windows and do further damage and, as problems escalate, because of the increase in criminal behaviour respectable residents leave. Wilson and Kelling suggest that to reduce crime, problems must be fixed when they are small, broken windows and building damage should be repaired quickly so that crime does not escalate and respectable residents do not leave. ⓐ

The broken windows theory can be applied to reduce crime. ⓑ For example, police can be asked to patrol on foot rather than in police cars. The safe and clean neighbourhoods programme found that residents in foot-patrolled neighbourhoods felt more secure and believed that crime had been reduced. ⓒ However, although residents felt safer actual crime rates were not reduced. ⓓ Another way the broken windows theory can be applied is to use the zero tolerance policing strategy that involves relentless and aggressive law enforcement against even minor crimes. A zero tolerance policing policy

---

suggests that minor crimes such as vandalism and littering must be pursued to prevent the escalation in criminal behaviour. In New York, a zero tolerance initiative cracked down on disorderly behaviour, public drinking, street prostitution and unsolicited windshield washing and crime rates fell by almost 40%. e

The broken windows theory suggests that social and environmental factors are the cause of crime. Sutherland would support this as he suggests that criminal behaviour is learned, and that a person becomes criminal because they adopt the norms and values of a criminal group in preference to the norms and values of non-criminal groups. f However, the application of the broken windows theory and a zero tolerance policing policy is unlikely to reduce crime caused by biological or cognitive factors. g

e **9/10 marks awarded.** This response demonstrates relevant knowledge and understanding and gives an accurate and detailed description. In a the student clearly and accurately describes the broken windows theory. In b, c, d and e the student makes clear, research-based suggestions as to how the broken windows theory can be applied to reduce crime. In f–g the student goes on to apply psychological evidence to evaluate the application of the broken windows theory. Point f could have been improved by explaining that if there are fewer criminal groups then criminal behaviour is less likely. The final point g is reasonable but is not fully explained and in any case was not needed. Overall, there is a well-developed line of reasoning which is clear and logically structured in the context of the question.

Student B

Wilson and Kelling suggest that if broken windows are not repaired vandals are likely to break more windows and that criminal behaviour will escalate and that to reduce crime broken windows and vandalised buildings should be repaired quickly so that crime does not escalate. a The broken windows theory can be applied to reduce crime by using the zero tolerance policing strategy that involves aggressive law enforcement against even minor crimes to prevent the escalation in criminal behaviour. b The broken windows theory suggests that social factors are the cause of crime. However, other psychologists have found that biological and/or cognitive factors cause crime. c

e **3–5/10 marks awarded.** The answer shows some relevant knowledge and understanding but is limited in description and lacking in detail. Point a lacks detail and is repetitive. Point b is a relevant application but is not supported by evidence. Point c could have been improved by making it relevant to the application of the broken windows theory to reduce crime. Overall, there is some evidence of selection of material to address the question but the answer demonstrates a limited application of psychological knowledge.

7   b*   Assess the usefulness of research into the social causes of crime.   (15 marks)

ⓔ The question injunction is 'assess'. This question assesses AO1 and AO3 skills.

AO1 (2 marks): You should demonstrate knowledge and understanding by accurately identifying what is meant by usefulness of research in terms of the social causes of crime. Note that there are only 2 marks for AO1 descriptive content.

AO3 (13 marks): Your answer should be an analysis, interpretation and evaluation of the usefulness of research into the social causes of crime. 'Usefulness' may include benefit, appropriateness, accuracy, application and methodological issues. Usefulness can include usefulness to psychology as an academic discipline and/or usefulness to society. Your answer could consider whether research into the social causes of crime has validity and/or reliability and you could also consider the usefulness of social research compared to alternative explanations for crime.

Student A

Psychological research has shown several different social causes for crime. In a longitudinal study, Farrington tested the hypothesis that nurture in problem families produces problem children and found that when the participants were age 20, twice as many of those with convicted fathers or convicted mothers had convictions compared to those without convicted fathers or mothers. **ⓐ** This research is **useful as it suggests** that families in which children are likely to become criminals can be identified and intervention strategies can be put in place to prevent the children turning to crime. **ⓑ However**, children inherit genes as well as social background from parents, and Farrington could not rule out the influence of genetic factors (nature) on criminal behaviour. **ⓒ**

Another useful theory relating to the social causes of crime is by Sutherland who suggests that through social interaction individuals learn the values, attitudes and techniques for criminal behaviour. According to Sutherland, a person becomes criminal because they adopt the norms and values of a criminal group in preference to the norms and values of non-criminal groups. **ⓓ** This **theory is useful** as it explains why crime rates among young people are high in urban areas in which criminal gangs 'hang out' on the streets. **ⓔ However**, it is important to remember that many children who grow up in criminogenic areas will not commit crimes. **ⓕ**

Research into the social causes of crime has looked at the effect of the social environment. According to Wilson and Kelling, if signs of decay, such as broken windows, are not repaired vandals are likely to commit further crimes and, as problems escalate, respectable residents leave the neighbourhood. **ⓖ** **Also**, according to Newman, broken windows and vandalism occur because communities do not care about the area and crime is reduced if neighbourhoods are designed as defensible spaces whose physical characteristics function to allow the residents to become responsible for ensuring security. ∎ **This research is useful** as it suggests that if environmental problems, such as building damage are repaired quickly crime will not escalate, and that careful design of the built environment can reduce crime. ∎

Perhaps the most useful aspect of research into the social causes of crime is that if nurture, rather than nature, is shown to be the cause of crime, applications to reduce crime can be developed because it is easier to change a person's situation than his or her biological characteristics. ∎ However, a wholly social explanation for crime is reductionist. Reductionism is the principle of analysing complex things into simple parts, for example, explaining complex criminal behaviour in terms of simplistic single factor causes, such as the social environment. Although reductionist hypotheses are easier to test, simplistic explanations such as social explanations for crime **are not always useful** because they may prevent further attempts to research more complex explanations. ∎ Also, research into the social causes of crime cannot explain individual differences in criminal behaviour. For example, some children who grow up in criminal families do not grow up to become criminals, and not everyone who lives in a 'broken' urban area commits crime so as well as looking at social causes it might be **useful if** psychologists carried out more research on the reasons why people do not commit crime. ∎

ⓔ **12/15 marks awarded.** This is a top band answer. It is explicitly related to the context of the question, shows good relevant knowledge and understanding and demonstrates points of analysis, interpretation and evaluation covering a range of issues. The argument is competently organised, balanced and well developed. There is effective use of examples showing good understanding and a well-developed line of reasoning which is clear and logically structured. In a–c, d–f and g–i the student outlines three different areas of research into the social causes of crime and explains how the research is useful and can be applied to reduce crime. In j and k the student relates the issue of nature vs nurture to the usefulness of research into the social causes of crime, and in l makes an effectively argued suggestion as to how to increase the usefulness of research.

Student B

Farrington tested family background as a social cause for crime and found that 48% of boys with convicted fathers also had convictions compared to 19% of those without convicted fathers. a This research is **useful as it suggests** that families in which children are likely to become criminals can be identified. b **However**, ethical issues arise when labelling families as likely to produce criminal children. c

Sutherland suggests that a person becomes a criminal because they interact with, and adopt the norms and values of, a criminal group. d This **theory is useful** as it explains why crime rates are high in criminal gangs in urban areas. e

> According to Wilson and Kelling, social causes of crime lie in the environment and if signs of decay, such as broken windows, are not repaired vandals are likely to commit further crimes and criminal behaviour will increase. **f** **This research is useful** as it suggests that if building damage is repaired quickly crime will not escalate. **g**
>
> However, a social explanation for crime is reductionist and simplistic explanations for crime **are not always useful** because they may overemphasise some causes and ignore other causes. **h** Also, research into the social causes of crime cannot explain individual differences in criminal behaviour. For example, some children who grow up in criminal families do not become criminals. **i**

e **4–7/15 marks awarded.** This answer is rather 'list like', but shows reasonable knowledge and understanding and includes a limited number of points of analysis, interpretation and evaluation. The points are mostly related to the context of the question. In **a–c** there is a very brief outline of the findings by Farrington, but neither of the evaluative points **b** and **c** are well explained. In **d** and **e**, the student gives a very brief outline of Sutherland's theory and states rather than explains its usefulness. In **f** and **g** the answer summarises the broken windows theory — but without naming it as such, and states rather than explains its usefulness. Finally, in **h–i** the student makes a point about reductionism and about individual differences, neither of which is argued or explained effectively.

It might be a useful exercise to compare this answer to the one by Student A, or to use this essay as a plan and see if you can rewrite it as a top-band answer.

On a run-down urban estate comprising mostly high-rise apartment blocks, many shops and houses are derelict, windows are broken and boarded up, gangs of youths 'hang out' on street corners, squatters live in abandoned buildings and muggings are frequent in the high-rise walkways.

7 c* **Discuss how the features of this urban neighbourhood may influence the crime rates.** (10 marks)

e The question injunction is 'discuss' and the question assesses AO2 skills. This question is worth 10 AO2 marks and you must apply knowledge and understanding of research into how features of the urban environment influence crime rates. For a top-band mark your answer must relate your points explicitly to the source question. You should be able to analyse how a range of features in an urban area may (or may not) influence the crime rate. Your answer could refer to any appropriate feature of an urban environment and consider how this may influence the crime rate. Your answer could also include an argument relating to the types of crime that may not be influenced by the environment, or analysis of how the issues of free will vs determinism and/or nature vs nurture can be applied to explain crime.

Student A

Are crimes committed because of the situation people are in or because of the sort of people criminals are? According to social psychologists, environmental factors influence crime, especially in urban areas. In the 'broken windows' theory, Wilson and Kelling suggest that crime will increase in neighbourhoods where vandalism occurs. They suggest that if signs of decay, such as broken windows, are not repaired vandals are likely to break more windows and do further damage and, as problems escalate, respectable residents leave because of the increase in criminal behaviour. [a] The source suggests that in this urban estate many shops and houses are derelict and windows are broken and boarded up. **If the theory of urban decay** leading to crime is correct then crime rates will escalate on the estate as respectable residents will move away leaving the estate to criminal gangs. [b] The high-rise blocks of apartments on the estate may also be a feature of the estate that influences the crime rate. [c] Supposed to represent 'ideal' modernist living, the huge Pruitt–Igoe estate became an icon of urban planning failure as the estate began to decline soon after its completion. Pruitt–Igoe was internationally infamous for poverty and crime, leading to its eventual demolition. [d] Wilson and Kelling would argue that had the estate's problems, such as broken windows, been fixed when they first appeared, crime would not have escalated. [e]

Another feature that may increase crime on this estate is that, according to the source 'gangs of youths hang out on street corners'. [f] Sutherland, argues that criminal behaviour is learned, and that a person becomes a criminal because they adopt the norms and values of a criminal group in preference to the norms and values of non-criminal groups. If this is correct then the young people who interact with the gangs may adopt the values of the criminal gang members. [g]

A third feature of the estate that may influence crime is the lack of defensible space. According to the source, 'squatters live in the abandoned buildings' and this indicates a lack of sense of ownership and responsibility for the property. [h] According to Newman, defensible space is a residential environment whose physical characteristics and building layout allow the residents to become responsible for their security. Newman argues that an area is safer when people feel a sense of ownership because when each space in an area is owned and cared for by a responsible party criminal intruders, aware they may be watched, are less likely. Clearly, in the source, estate criminals do not feel 'watched' as many spaces are 'derelict and boarded up' for which no one feels responsible. [i]

However, to suggest that the features of the estate cause all crime is quite a deterministic and simplistic environmental explanation. [j] Most psychologists would argue that people have the free will to choose whether to engage in crime or not, and many people who grow up on deprived urban estates do not engage in crime. Perhaps the broken and derelict features of the urban estate only influence, or even facilitate, the rate of crime in those individuals who would have engaged in crime wherever they lived? [k]

ⓔ 9/10 marks awarded. This is a top-band answer. It demonstrates an explicit, accurate and relevant application of psychological knowledge and understanding to the question. There is a well-developed line of reasoning which is clear and logically structured. In ⓐ, ⓑ, ⓒ, ⓓ and ⓔ there is a detailed and effectively explained argument applying the broken windows theory explicitly to the source. The inclusion of the Pruitt–Igoe and mention of the high-rise nature are strengths of this answer. In ⓕ and ⓖ the student picks up the source's mention of 'gangs' as a feature of the estate and relates this to the theory of learning by social interaction. In ⓗ and ⓘ the student discusses the theory of defensible space, linking this to the squatters in the abandoned buildings and explaining why lack of defensible space may encourage criminality. Finally, in ⓙ and ⓚ the student argues a point about environmental determinism suggesting that people have the free will to choose whether to commit crime or not. **A strength of the answer is that each point is related and explained in the context of the source for the question.**

Student B

The broken windows theory suggests that if signs of decay, such as broken windows, are not repaired vandals are likely to break more windows and do further damage and crime rates will escalate. ⓐ **If this theory** is correct then on the estate, because there is derelict property and boarded-up windows, crime rates will rise. ⓑ **Another feature** that may increase crime on this estate is that 'gangs of youths hang out on street corners'. ⓒ Sutherland, argues that a person becomes a criminal because they adopt the norms and values of a criminal group and if this is correct then the young people who hang around with the gangs will also engage in criminal behaviour. ⓓ

However, cognitive psychologists would argue that people have the free will to choose whether to engage in crime or not, and perhaps crime on the estate is high because those who choose not to be criminals have moved away? ⓔ

ⓔ 5–6/10 marks awarded. This is a low/mid-band answer. It demonstrates a limited application of psychological knowledge and understanding. In ⓐ–ⓑ the student applies the theory of broken windows to the question of crime on the urban estate, but the point made is stated rather than being explained and discussed. Likewise, in ⓒ–ⓓ the student applies the theory of learned behaviour to the question of crime on the estate but the point made lacks explanation. In ⓔ the student applies the issue of free will to the question of crime on the estate, suggesting an alternative reason why crime will occur. The information presented is relevant and is supported by limited evidence which is related to the source and question.

It might be a useful exercise to compare this answer to the one by Student A, or to use this essay as a plan and see if you can rewrite it as a top-band answer.

Option 3: environmental psychology

In Section B every question requires a synoptic response and you must answer all parts of the question.

8 a* Using the research by Black and Black (2007) explain how environmental stressors impact our biological responses.

(10 marks)

ⓔ The question injunction is 'explain'. This question assesses AO1 and AO2 skills.

AO1 (5 marks): You must refer to the key study by Black and Black (2007) to access the top band. Knowledge and understanding should be demonstrated through describing the psychological evidence of the key study appropriately and effectively.

AO2 (5 marks): You should apply knowledge and understanding of the Black and Black (2007) study to explain how environmental stressors impact our biological responses. It is important for your answer to make the link between environmental stressors and biological states. An answer that simply describes the study without an explanation will only be awarded marks in the lower bands.

Student A

Research shows that environmental factors may cause stress. One environmental stressor is noise and sudden and unexpected noise produces biological responses of increased blood pressure and increased heart rate. Even when a person is accustomed to an environment in which noise levels are high, physiological changes occur. **a** Black and Black researched the impact of aircraft noise on community health in residential areas near Sydney airport and in a matched control area unaffected by aircraft noise — 750 participants were sent a survey in both the aircraft noise area and in the control area. Also, noise stations were set up outside randomly selected households in the aircraft noise area and in the control area. The survey collected data on health-related quality of life and noise stress and a critical question asked 'Have you ever been told by a doctor that you have high blood pressure?' **b** The research concluded that people who have been chronically exposed to high aircraft noise levels are more likely to report stress and hypertension compared with those not exposed to aircraft noise. **c** This research shows how an environmental stressor, such as aircraft noise, impacts biological responses, and for those who live near an airport, because the noise caused by aircraft will continue, the stress will be long term. **d** Because stress causes raised heart rate and high blood pressure, long-term stress can damage blood vessels which may lead to stroke or heart attacks. Also, the stress hormone, cortisol, can cause damage to health because raised cortisol levels reduce our immune function and also increase the risk of depression and mental illness. **e**

ⓔ 9–10 marks awarded. This is a top-band answer which demonstrates relevant knowledge and understanding. In **a** the student gives an accurate description of noise as an environmental stressor. In **b** the student gives a detailed and accurate description of the research by Black and Black. In c, d and e the student explains how the Black and Black conclusion relates to environmental stressors and changes in biological states. There is appropriate selection of material to address the question and the answer demonstrates good application of psychological knowledge and understanding to the question. There is a well-developed line of reasoning which is clear and logically structured.

Student B

One environmental stressor is sudden noise that produces biological responses of increased blood pressure and increased heart rate. a Black and Black sent a survey to people who were either affected by aircraft noise or who were not. The questionnaire collected data on health and a critical question asked 'Have you ever been told by a doctor that you have high blood pressure?' The mean scores of general and mental health of the noise group were lower than the control group suggesting that noise exposure did impact health. b It was concluded that people who have been exposed to aircraft noise are more likely to report stress and hypertension. c This shows how an environmental stressor impacts biological responses because noise is an environmental stressor and long-term stress can damage blood vessels, leading to stroke or heart attacks. d

e **5–6/10 marks awarded.** The answer demonstrates relevant knowledge and understanding, but the description and explanation, though accurate, lack detail. In a–b and c there is some evidence of selection of material to address the question and in d there is a brief explanation as to how environmental stress influences biological response. Overall, the answer demonstrates a reasonable application of psychological knowledge and understanding to the question. The information presented is in the most part relevant and supported by some evidence.

8 b* Assess the methodological issues involved when researching the impact of environmental stressors on biological responses.   (15 marks)

e The question injunction is 'assess'. This question assesses AO1 and AO3 skills

AO1 (2 marks): You can demonstrate knowledge and understanding by identifying issues such as how to identify environmental stressors, how and what to measure as the effect of environmental stressors and how to gain an unbiased sample. Note that there are only 2 marks available for AO1 descriptive content.

AO3 (13 marks): You must apply your knowledge and understanding of the methodological issues involved when researching the impact of environmental stressors. These issues must be specifically linked to the question. Responses could consider any appropriate methodological issues such as the methodology used, validity, reliability and generalisability. You can also discuss the issue of whether it is the situation or the disposition of people that causes stress, and the difficulty of separating situational from dispositional factors. Support your points by using examples of research evidence and always explain your points fully. For a top-band mark try to identify and argue at least four points.

Student A

Ethical issues arise when researching the impact of environmental stressors on biological responses because informed consent is needed before collecting and analysing biological samples such as heart rate, blood or urine. a Although objective biological evidence may give a valid measure of levels of cortisol and adrenalin, **samples are likely to be small**. Small samples are not representative of a larger population and when small samples are used in research into the effects of environmental stress generalisability is low. b

When using self-report to research the impact of environmental stressors **the issue of gaining a valid measure arises** because much research into stress involves asking people to complete questionnaires. c **An advantage** of using self-report methods is that can data can be collected from a large sample of people quite quickly so that the results can be generalised to the target population. For example in the Black and Black research 1,500 participants were sent questionnaires — 750 in the aircraft noise condition and 750 in the control (no noise) condition. d **Another advantage** of using self-report to measure the impact of environmental stressors is that questionnaires can gather qualitative data first hand which allows people's personal attitudes to be assessed. e The Black and Black questionnaire measured seven characteristics, including quality of life, noise stress and confounding factors such as smoking. They also gathered quantitative data by measuring hypertension using a closed critical question. f

However, using self-report to measure the effects of environmental stressors may raise a methodological issue as people may misunderstand questions, may not tell the truth or may give socially desirable answers, all of which reduce the validity of the results. g For example, the participants in the Black and Black research were reported to be sharply annoyed by the aircraft noise and thus may have overestimated the impact of noise on their health. Also, in the Black and Black study, we cannot rely on the responses to the critical question as a valid measure of hypertension, because we only know how many of the sample 'knew' they were hypertensive, and many of them, both in the noise condition and in the control condition may not have known they had raised blood pressure. h **That said, using an experimental method** with a control group allows researchers to make cause-and-effect statements about the effect of environmental stressors on biological responses. An advantage of the Black and Black research is the use of the no noise control group so that comparisons could be made between the health of people living in aircraft noise conditions and those who did not. i

Another methodological issue arises when measuring the effect of environmental stressors such as noise or temperature. Even if research finds hypertension, or stress hormones, in participants, can they be certain that these biological changes are a direct result of environmental stress and that no other variables, such as lack of sleep, or stress at work, caused the biological changes? j In everyday life, there are many sources of stress and research has also shown that work, especially shift work can also cause a biological stress response, and it may be impossible to separate the impact of environmental stressors from other causes of stress. k

Also, **much research** into the impact of environmental stressors **ignores individual differences** in how people respond to stressors and some people may be more stressed by noise than others. ⬛ The Selye model of the response to stressors takes a reductionist biological approach suggesting no free will or individual differences in how people cope with stressors, but stress is a complex subject and what causes stress in one person may not cause stress in another. ⬛ For example, seasonal changes in light cause seasonal affective disorder (SAD) in only a minority of people. **Reductionist research** that only looks at situational variables in the environment as a cause of stress, ignoring the characteristics of the individuals involved, may overemphasise environmental factors as a cause of biological responses. ⬛

ⓔ **13–15/15 marks awarded.** Student A has written an extremely effective, top-band answer. It is explicitly related to the context of the question, shows good relevant knowledge and understanding and demonstrates points of analysis, interpretation and evaluation covering a range of issues. The argument is competently organised, balanced and well developed. There is effective use of examples showing good understanding and a well-developed line of reasoning which is clear and logically structured. In a–b, c–d, and e–f the student clearly explains three methodological issues arising when researching the impact of environmental variables on biological responses and these issues are clearly explained and supported by relevant evidence. In g, h and i the answer, still focused on the issue of validity, continues the argument by making alternative points, all relevant to the question. In j, k, l, m and n the answer links methodological issues to the question of situation or disposition as a cause of stress and also relates the issue of reductionism and free will to the question. All points are explained well and supported by a wide range of appropriate evidence. Throughout the answer there is effective use of examples and valid conclusions are drawn, showing good understanding. However, this is a long answer, and had the student only written the content in c–k a top-band mark would still probably have been awarded.

Student B

Using self-report **raises the issue of validity** because much research into stress involves asking people to complete questionnaires. ⬛ **An advantage** of using self-report methods is that can data can be collected from a large sample of people quite quickly so that the results can be generalised to the target population. For example, in the Black and Black research 1,500 participants were sent questionnaires. ⬛ **Another advantage** of using self-report to measure the impact of environmental stressors is that questionnaires can gather qualitative data first hand and the Black and Black questionnaire obtained data from participants that could not have been gained without asking them. ⬛

However, using self-report may reduce validity because people may give socially desirable answers. ⬛ For example, the participants in the Black and Black research who were annoyed by aircraft noise may have overestimated the impact of noise on their health. Also, in the Black and Black study, the critical question may not be a valid measure of high blood pressure as some participants may not have known they had raised blood pressure. **e** But an advantage of the Black and Black research is the use of **experimental methods and a control group** so that comparisons could be made between the people living in aircraft noise conditions and those who did not experience aircraft noise. **f**

Another methodological issue arises because even if researchers find hypertension, or stress hormones, in participants, they cannot be sure that these biological changes are a direct result of environmental stress. **g** Research has shown that work, especially shift work, can cause a biological stress response, and it may be impossible to separate the impact of environmental stressors from other causes of stress. **h**

e 6–7/15 marks awarded. The answer demonstrates relevant knowledge and understanding, but makes a limited range of points of analysis, interpretation and evaluation. The main body of the argument in **a–f** considers the issue of self-report/validity and includes only the Black and Black study as supporting evidence. This could be read as an evaluation of the Black and Black study rather than an answer to the question of methodological issues involved when researching the impact of environmental stressors on biological responses. The point in **g** and **h** is quite well focused on the question but could be more clearly linked to a methodological issue. There is a line of reasoning presented with some structure, and the information presented is accurate but could be made more relevant to the context of the question.

Residents living in a community under the flight path of a busy airport are complaining of lack of sleep and generally poor health and have formed an association to protest against the construction of a new runway. Their protest is supported by a local GP who says 'there is a high incidence of physical and mental health problems in local people'.

8 c* Discuss how psychologists might apply their knowledge of environmental stress to explain how living near a busy airport may impact the health of residents.

(10 marks)

e The question injunction is 'discuss' and the question assesses AO2 skills. You must apply your knowledge and understanding of research into how environmental stressors impact health. For a top-band mark your answer must relate your points explicitly to the source in the question. You should be able to analyse how living near a busy airport may, or may not, influence health. Your answer should demonstrate understanding of the biological effects of stress and consider how this may influence health. Your answer could also include an argument that there are causes of ill health other than environmental factors and the issue of situational vs dispositional factors, and you could also mention reductionism.

Student A

To explain how living near a busy airport may impact the health of residents, **psychologists must explain** the biological response to stressors and show how living near an airport may cause stress. a Selye suggests that when we perceive a stressor, adrenaline and stress hormones are released into the bloodstream, and that the heart rate increases, blood pressure rises and muscles tense in response. Selye proposes that if a stressor continues for a long time, the body is unable to cope and the immune system may be damaged and stress-related diseases, such as high blood pressure and depression, are likely to occur. b **Psychologists must explain to the airport owners** that environmental stressors, such as sudden and unexpected noise produces increased blood pressure and increased heart rate and that the health of the residents living under the flight path may be affected by aircraft noise. c **To convince the owners** of the airport, the research by Black and Black, should be explained. Black and Black, who researched the impact of aircraft noise on community health, found that the mean scores of general health and mental health of the noise exposure group were significantly lower than in a matched control group and concluded that people who are chronically exposed to high aircraft noise levels are more likely to report stress and hypertension. d

These findings can be used to persuade managers of airports to restrict noisy flights to day times. Before a new runway is built, designers of aircraft should be asked to invest in manufacturing planes with quieter engines. Also, residents should be helped and the homes and offices near airports should be insulated, as far as possible, from noise by triple glazing and by the use of noise resistant materials. e

However, the owners of the airport are likely to argue that many in the community are in good health and that the health problems of some residents cannot be proved to be caused by aircraft noise. They are likely to argue against paying for noise insulation by suggesting that psychological research also shows that work or everyday hassles also cause stress-related ill health and that it is impossible to 'prove' the extent to which the aircraft noise is a cause of ill health in the community. f **If possible, the protesting** residents should insist that before a new runway is built an experimental study should be carried out to measure the decibel level and frequency of aircraft noise in the area, and to compare the health of residents in their community with that of a community not affected by aircraft noise. g

e **9/10 marks awarded.** This is a top-band answer. It demonstrates an explicit, accurate and relevant application of psychological knowledge and understanding to the question. There is a well-developed line of reasoning which is clear and logically structured. In a, b, c and d there is a detailed and effectively explained argument applying research into how stress affects health and how aircraft noise affects health to the source. The evidence included in c and d is a strength as it is explicitly related to the context of the question. In e the answer makes suggestions as to how the impact of aircraft noise can be reduced and in f the student shows understanding of methodological issues and relates this to the question. Finally, in g the student makes a sensible suggestion for further research to help the residents. **A strength of the answer is that each point is related and explained in the context of the source for the question.**

Student B

Psychologists have found that environmental stressors, such as sudden and unexpected noise produces increased blood pressure and increased heart rate and that long-term exposure to stressors leads to ill health. a Black and Black, who researched the impact of aircraft noise on community health, found that the general health and mental health of the noise exposure group was lower than in a matched control group and concluded that people who are exposed to high aircraft noise levels are more likely to report stress and hypertension. b **These findings can be used to persuade managers of airports** not to allow noisy flights during the night and to pay for insulation in homes near the airport to reduce the effect of noise. c **However**, the owners of the airport are likely to argue that the health problems of some residents may be caused by other factors and that psychologists cannot 'prove' that aircraft noise is a cause of ill health in the community. d

e **5/10 marks awarded.** This answer demonstrates a limited application of psychological knowledge and understanding to the question. In a and b the answer is descriptive AO1 rather than analytical AO2 and it is not until point c that the evidence is applied to the question. In d, which is a statement rather than an explanation, the answer does demonstrate some understanding of a counter-argument, but this could have been expanded and supported by evidence.

It might be a useful exercise to compare this answer to the one by Student A, or to use this essay as a plan and see if you can rewrite it as a top-band answer.

Knowledge check answers

Issues in mental health

1 In institutionalised care a person with a mental illness is separated from society and admitted to a psychiatric institution to be treated. In community-based mental healthcare a person with a mental illness is treated and cared for 'at home' in the community.

2 Labelling people as abnormal is unethical because psychiatric labels are 'sticky' and if labelled as abnormal people could be treated differently and unfairly, perhaps lose employment opportunities and may be forced to have treatment.

3 To verify a diagnosis a second psychiatrist should be asked to make an independent diagnosis. If both diagnoses are the same then the diagnosis can be said to be reliable.

4 The participants, who were unaware they were being observed, were the doctors, nurses, ward staff and patients in 12 psychiatric hospitals in 5 US states. The participant observers were 8 people who acted as 'pseudo-patients', 5 men and 3 women of various ages and occupations.

5 This behaviour is the sign of an anxiety disorder, probably OCD because people with OCD experience recurrent, unwanted thoughts and compulsive repetitive behaviours, such as in Sigmund's case repeatedly checking and relocking the door.

6 A biochemical explanation for schizophrenia is an excess of the neurotransmitter dopamine. A biochemical explanation for depression is an imbalance in the neurotransmitter serotonin.

7 Close relatives of someone with depression, especially identical twins, have a higher than average risk of developing depression. Harrington et al. (1993) found that about 20% of close relatives of people with depression also suffer from depression compared to about 10% of the general population.

8 The medical model suggests that mental illness is caused by biochemistry, genetics and/or brain anatomy and thus that our biological nature (not nurture) causes mental illness.

9 Drugs can be used to treat the affective disorder depression. For example, SSRI drugs can be used as these drugs stop the reuptake of serotonin and due to increased levels of the neurotransmitter serotonin in the synapse the patient's mood is enhanced.

10 The behaviourist explanation assumes that abnormal behaviour is learned in the same way as normal behaviour and that it can be unlearned. The cognitive approach proposes that abnormal behaviour is caused by mental processes when people make incorrect inferences about themselves or others, and/or have negative thoughts about themselves and the future.

11 The diagnosis of mental illness is not the same as the diagnosis of a physical illness. A broken leg is not a matter of opinion, but because many mental illnesses are not caused by biological factors it is difficult to gain scientific measurements of the causes of dysfunctional behaviour. As a result, in contrast to the way a physical illness is diagnosed, 'subjective opinion' is involved in deciding whether behaviour is considered as normal or abnormal and whether or not a person is mentally ill and requires treatment.

12 Behaviourist therapies based on operant conditioning assume that behaviour can be relearned and that behaviour that brings about pleasurable consequences will be repeated. In behaviour modification treatments, positive reinforcement is used where desired behaviour is rewarded by a pleasant consequence. Behaviour modification programmes are used to change the behaviour of people who are 'rewarded' for behaving in an acceptable manner.

Criminal psychology

13 Social factors: upbringing and learning from other people. Cognitive factors: morality and thinking patterns.

14 Raine found differences in the brains of murderers compared to 'normal' people, for example, reduced activity in the prefrontal cortex, reduced activity in the corpus callosum and abnormal asymmetries in the amygdala. The prefrontal area of the brain has been associated with impulsivity, and damage to the corpus callosum has been associated with a predisposition to violence, so these findings support the suggestion that biological factors may explain why some people commit violent crimes.

15 In fingerprint analysis motivating factors may include personal job satisfaction and the positive emotional effects associated with matching fingerprints when a serious crime is involved. When analysing unclear fingerprints the emotional 'need' to find the criminal and fear of making a mistake may motivate the investigator to wrongly 'identify' the fingerprint.

16 Possible suggestions:
   - To reduce emotional bias the forensic scientist is not told not what type of crime has been committed.
   - The fingerprint investigator's job performance is not judged on his/her positive identification 'hit rate'.
   - Independent checking is always carried out.
   - The forensic scientist has no contact with the police investigation.

17 Possible reasons:
- Asking a witness to recall an incident from a variety of perspectives may activate multiple pathways to memory retrieval which may trigger forgotten details of the incident.
- Asking a witness to reconstruct the physical and personal context of the incident may provide contextual cues that were encoded with the memory and these context cues may activate the memory of the incident.

18 Deception, manipulation, pressure, intimidation and leading questions.

19 Training in the use of the cognitive interview is important because training can improve the confidence and ability of a police officer. Interviewers need basic social skills in communicating effectively with witnesses and need to be able to develop rapport with witnesses before the interview starts.

20 Dispositional characteristics.

21 According to Newman, defensible space is a residential environment whose physical characteristics, building layout and plan, function to allow inhabitants to become the key agents in ensuring their security.

22 Zero tolerance is a policing strategy that involves aggressive law enforcement against even minor crimes such as graffiti and littering because it is easier to prevent a slide into crime than to rescue a neighbourhood when criminality is established.

23 The deprivation model suggests that it is the situational factors of the prison that account for aggression and that the experience of imprisonment causes inmates frustration which leads to aggression, but the importation model suggests that offenders enter prison with characteristics, such as personality traits and values, that predict they are more likely to engage in aggressive behaviours.

Environmental psychology

24 When we are stressed the sympathetic branch of the nervous system stimulates the adrenal gland to release adrenaline, noradrenaline and corticosteroids into the bloodstream. These physiological changes cause the 'flight-or-fight' response symptoms such as increased heart rate and blood pressure and a dry mouth.

25 When we are stressed, the ability of the immune system to protect us against antigens is reduced. This is called the immune-suppressive effect of stress. In long-term stress increased levels of corticosteroids reduce the production of antibodies (natural killer cells) that help to protect against viruses.

26 Temperature, noise, crowding.

27 One advantage is that a large sample was used and the use of a control group who were unaffected by aircraft noise gave the research a comparison group. One disadvantage is that Black and Black used self-report. Because the participants were aware the study was on environmental noise, social desirability bias may have occurred where those living near the airport may have overestimated the nuisance and distress caused by the aircraft noise.

28 Circadian rhythms are cycles of behaviour that happen every 24 hours. Infradian rhythms occur over a period of time greater than 24 hours. Ultradian rhythms repeat over a period of less than 24 hours.

29 A forward shift rotation (nights then mornings then afternoons) to phase delay the sleep-wake cycle and working each shift stage for 21 days will allow the body clock time to adjust.

30 Although this is a negative message, the message will be effective because the bad news is given with concrete information about what to do.

31 Positive appeal messages gave the most favourable levels of beliefs towards recycling, when given with personal and advertising message sources. The greatest increase in recycling behaviour came from the negative message presented by a personal acquaintance.

32 Cognitive load refers to the total amount of mental effort being used in the working memory.

33 The Hawthorne effect happens when people perform better when they are participants in an experiment because they change their behaviour due to the attention they are receiving rather than because of any manipulation of variables.

34 When designing a visual display, reduction of visual clutter and colour coding and geometric shapes as well as 'chunking' like information together can be used to make information easier to read.

35 High rises are less satisfactory than other housing forms for most people, social relations are more impersonal, helping behaviour is reduced and crime and fear of crime are greater.

36 One advantage is the high external (ecological) validity because this is a field experiment in which all patients had the same surgery and they were matched on age, weight and floor level. The patients were all recovering from the same surgery and the only difference was whether they viewed the nature scene or the brick wall.

37 Social distance zone is the personal space between 1.5 and 3 m. It is the most comfortable zone to start a conversation between people who do not know each other well. For example, it is the distance you keep from strangers like shopkeepers, service providers, the postman etc.

38 Employees in open-plan offices dislike not having sound privacy, they dislike not having enough space or private space and they dislike not being able to concentrate because of noise levels and interruptions.

Index